Gods, Goddesses, and Pharaohs of Ancient Egypt

An Enthralling Overview of Deities in Egyptian Mythology and Powerful Rulers Who Shaped the Land of the Nile

© Copyright 2025 - All rights reserved.

The content contained within this book may not be reproduced, duplicated, or transmitted without direct written permission from the author or the publisher.

Under no circumstances will any blame or legal responsibility be held against the publisher, or author, for any damages, reparation, or monetary loss due to the information contained within this book, either directly or indirectly.

Legal Notice:

This book is copyright protected. It is only for personal use. You cannot amend, distribute, sell, use, quote, or paraphrase any part, or the content within this book, without the consent of the author or publisher.

Disclaimer Notice:

Please note the information contained within this document is for educational and entertainment purposes only. All effort has been executed to present accurate, up-to-date, reliable, and complete information. No warranties of any kind are declared or implied. Readers acknowledge that the author is not engaging in the rendering of legal, financial, medical, or professional advice. The content within this book has been derived from various sources. Please consult a licensed professional before attempting any techniques outlined in this book.

By reading this document, the reader agrees that under no circumstances is the author responsible for any losses, direct or indirect, that are incurred as a result of the use of the information contained within this document, including, but not limited to, errors, omissions, or inaccuracies.

Free limited time bonus

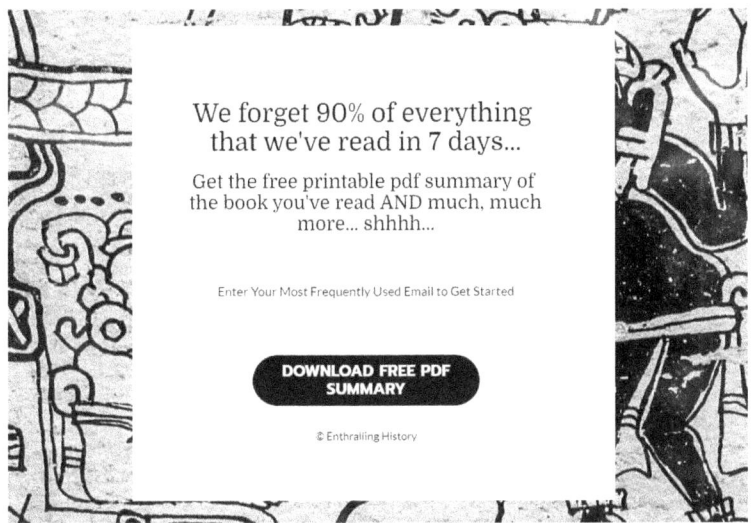

Stop for a moment. We have a free bonus set up for you. The problem is this: we forget 90% of everything that we read after 7 days. Crazy fact, right? Here's the solution: we've created a printable, 1-page pdf summary for this book that you're reading now. All you have to do to get your free pdf summary is to go to the following website:
https://livetolearn.lpages.co/enthrallinghistory/

Or, Scan the QR code!

Once you do, it will be intuitive. Enjoy, and thank you!

Table of Contents

PART 1: GODS AND GODDESSES OF ANCIENT EGYPT 1
    INTRODUCTION 3
    CHAPTER 1: THE ORIGINS OF EGYPTIAN MYTHOLOGY 5
    CHAPTER 2: THE SUN AND THE SKY: RA AND NUT 11
    CHAPTER 3: CHAOS AND ORDER: SET AND OSIRIS 22
    CHAPTER 4: LOVE AND MAGIC: ISIS 31
    CHAPTER 5: THE GOD OF MUMMIFICATION: ANUBIS 40
    CHAPTER 6: THE GUARDIANS OF ORDER: THOTH AND MA'AT 50
    CHAPTER 7: HORUS THE FALCON KING 60
    CHAPTER 8: SERPENT MAGIC AND TRANSFORMATION: WADJET AND SOBEK 68
    CHAPTER 9: LESSER-KNOWN DEITIES: A CASE STUDY 79
    CHAPTER 10: THE IMPACT OF EGYPTIAN MYTHOLOGY ON MODERN CULTURE 91
    CONCLUSION 96

PART 2: PHARAOHS OF ANCIENT EGYPT 99
    INTRODUCTION 101
    CHAPTER 1: EARLY PHARAOHS: THE FIRST DYNASTIC PERIOD 104
    CHAPTER 2: THE PHARAOHS OF THE OLD KINGDOM 119
    CHAPTER 3: PHARAOHS OF THE MIDDLE KINGDOM 133
    CHAPTER 4: HATSHEPSUT AND AKHENATEN 145
    CHAPTER 5: THE BOY KING: TUTANKHAMUN'S REIGN AND HIS TOMB 157

CHAPTER 6: RAMESSES II THE GREAT: A PHARAOH'S LEGACY 163

CHAPTER 7: MYSTERIES OF THE MUMMIES: DEATH AND AFTERLIFE OF THE PHARAOHS 173

CHAPTER 8: THE LATE PERIOD AND THE END OF PHARAONIC RULE 178

CHAPTER 9: THE INFLUENCE AND LEGACY OF ANCIENT EGYPT'S RULERS 187

CONCLUSION 191

PHARAOHS, DYNASTIES, AND DATES 194

HERE'S ANOTHER BOOK BY ENTHRALLING HISTORY THAT YOU MIGHT LIKE 217

FREE LIMITED TIME BONUS 218

BIBLIOGRAPHY 219

IMAGE SOURCES 222

Part 1: Gods and Goddesses of Ancient Egypt

An Enthralling Overview of the Most Important Deities in Egyptian Mythology

Introduction

From the towering pyramids touching the sky to the mysterious Sphinx guarding the vast Giza Plateau, the symbols of ancient Egypt have long captivated the imagination of the world. Yet, beyond these popular monuments lies a realm even more fascinating: the pantheon of Egyptian gods and goddesses. Many may be familiar with names like Osiris, Isis, Anubis, and Ra, perhaps from a passing reference in a movie, a depiction in a comic strip, or as dramatic characters in a fantasy novel. However, the true essence of these deities is far more complex and compelling than these modern interpretations often suggest.

Just as Norse and Greek mythologies are preserved in poems or hymns, the heart of Egyptian mythology also beats in texts. The Book of the Dead, the Pyramid Texts, and the Coffin Texts are a few examples of the ancient manuscripts that offer us a window into the Egyptian understanding of the cosmos, the afterlife, and the divine.

The ancient Egyptians did not see their gods and goddesses as mere symbols or abstract concepts; they were integral to every part of their lives, from the flooding of the Nile to the changing of seasons and from birth to death. Because of this, they took extreme care to please the divine, hoping their offerings and dedications could steer them away from the wrath of the gods. There was a time when they once abandoned a shrine of a mighty god. Perhaps as a punishment, the Egyptians had to go through seven years of drought and famine. Surprisingly, the event of the drought was historically correct and recorded in the Famine Stela excavated near Aswan.

Moreover, the relationship between these gods and goddesses reflects the intricacies of human relationships. The legend of Osiris's resurrection, for instance, unfolds not only a tale of betrayal and power struggle but also provides valuable lessons surrounding the themes of love, order, and the cycle of life. Similarly, the rivalry between Horus and Set mirrors the human struggles between order and chaos and good and evil.

To put it simply, understanding Egyptian mythology offers more than just a glimpse into ancient beliefs; it also provides a window into the worldview of one of the most fascinating civilizations in human history. It unveils how the ancient Egyptians interpreted the world around them, how they made sense of natural phenomena, and how they sought to understand their place in the vast universe.

This book aims to unravel the intricate web of stories, legends, and beliefs that form the Egyptian pantheon. It delves into the origins of the world according to Egyptian lore, the roles of various gods and goddesses of the pantheon—from the most famous ones to less-prominent and nearly forgotten deities—and their journeys and adventures in a time long past. Through this book, readers will discover the layers of each deity's nature, including how gods like Sobek are embodiments of protection and fertility and why a god was often seen as unpredictable. Of course, there will be a few details and legends you may already know, but there will hopefully be something waiting inside this book that might surprise you.

Chapter 1: The Origins of Egyptian Mythology

The story of how the world came to be cannot be explained in just a single page. While some believe it all began with an empty canvas or perhaps a dark expanse of nothingness, others chose not to describe the beginning at all, believing that the origin was too sacred and complex or too unknowable to be spoken aloud. The ancient Egyptians, however, thought otherwise. They had three narratives to explain the genesis of everything.

Those who hailed from the once glimmering city of the sun, Heliopolis, believed that everything started with the god Atum, who carved out the world from a primordial hill. Those in Memphis, on the other hand, held the god of craftsmen, Ptah, in high regard, while Egyptians in Hermopolis believed that the creation of the world had something to do with the Ogdoad, eight deities who existed in perfect balance with each other.

The Heliopolitan Creation Myth

Of course, just like other creation stories from various civilizations across the globe, the ancient Egyptians also believed that their story began with a vast expanse of nothingness where silence reigned supreme. According to this version, the first stirrings of creation began in the ancient city of Heliopolis. Once a major city of the ancient kingdom, it had been occupied as early as the time of prehistoric Egypt. However, the name Heliopolis was Greek (it means the "city of the sun"). To the ancient Egyptians, the city was known as Lunu, which translates to the "pillar city."

The city was of great importance. According to their beliefs, Heliopolis was the location where the sun's rays first kissed the earth and where legends of their gods and goddesses first unfolded.

Long before the land was dotted with obelisks and grand temples with towering statues, there existed only Nun, the primordial waters of chaos. These waters, dark and unfathomable, held within them the potential of all that was to be. In this boundless sea of possibility, an event would take place that would change the course of existence forever: the emergence of the very first piece of land, a sacred mound rising from the depths of Nun.

Atum, who later merged with the sun god Ra to become Atum-Ra, the first and most ancient of the Egyptian gods, came into being upon this mound. However, Atum, in his solitude, yearned for more than just existence. He yearned for life, for creation, and for the company of others.

And so, in a feat of divine power, Atum began the act of creation. From his own essence, he brought forth the first pair of deities: Shu, the god of air, and Tefnut, the goddess of moisture. Shu, with his breath of life, then filled the space between the heavens and the earth, while Tefnut brought the principle of order, weaving it delicately into the canvas of creation.

At one point, Shu and Tefnut were said to have disappeared when they went to explore the primeval waters, leaving Atum alone yet again. Perhaps desperate to cure his sadness and find his children, Atum sent forth the Eye of Ra (a divine entity often depicted as either the sun disk or the right Wedjat eye), which scholars often interpret to be synonymous with the goddess Hathor in certain myths.

The Eye of Ra was powerful and all-seeing. It journeyed through the chaos of Nun, illuminating the shadows and peering into the hidden crevices of the primordial sea. Back in the world, Atum waited, his heart heavy with worry and longing.

The Eye of Ra was successful in its quest. It returned with Shu and Tefnut to the sacred mound of creation. Atum's heart swelled with joy and relief. Overcome with happiness at the return of his children, tears streamed from his eyes, falling upon the fertile earth of the mound. From these tears of joy, something miraculous

Symbol of the Eye of Ra.[1]

occurred. Where each tear touched the earth, the dirt transformed, taking shape and life. These droplets also became the first humans.

Shu and Tefnut then gave birth to more divine beings. Geb was the god of the earth, while Nut was the goddess of the sky. Now, in ancient Egyptian beliefs, unions between siblings were common. For gods and mortal royals, it was thought to be a way to preserve their sacred lineage. And so, despite being siblings, Geb and Nut were joined as a divine couple. It was through them that the fundamental structure of the world was finally established. Geb (the earth) and Nut (the heavens above) were forever bound but eternally separated by their father, Shu.

However, Geb and Nut were not barren. Their union led to the birth of four more children, each with destinies that would further shape the world. Osiris was the firstborn son who soon became crowned the first king of Egypt. His position was not permanent, as he would embark on a journey to transform into the ruler of the underworld. Their second child was Isis, who was also the wife of Osiris. She was hailed as the goddess of magic and healing, and her wisdom was said to be as deep as the Nile itself. The third was Set, the god of chaos and storms. Although often thought to have brought destruction, Set was also crucial in bringing change, balance, and renewal. Last but not least was the goddess Nephthys. The wife of Set, Nephthys was associated with mourning and the protective care of the dead.

Along with Atum, Shu, Tefnut, Geb, and Nut, these nine gods formed the Great Ennead. They completed the creation of the world in their own ways. While Osiris introduced knowledge of agriculture, teaching mankind the ways of planting and harvesting to ensure their survival, Isis shared her sacred knowledge of magic. The goddess taught humans the art of medicine, as well as the ways of domestication. Set, on the other hand, had a complex role in shaping the world. He brought storms and upheavals. These were not always a form of destruction; they also served as a form of renewal and necessary disruption. Challenging the order of things was the only way to ensure that balance could be restored and maintained. Meanwhile, his wife, Nephthys, played a quieter role. She provided solace to the souls in the afterlife, ensuring their safe passage to the beyond.

The Memphite Creation Myth

While Atum was the main figure of the Heliopolis creation myth, this next tale of creation revolved around Ptah, the patron god of craftsmen and architects. In contrast to the story of Atum and the Heliopolis, this particular creation myth focused more on the power of the mind and speech.

Ptah was the patron god of Memphis. According to Memphite theology, the god created the world simply using his heart and tongue. Of course, this is not to be taken literally; he did not sacrifice his body parts to shape the world, like how the Norse god Odin created the world using the body of the primordial frost giant, Ymir. The ancient Egyptians held strong to the belief that the heart was the very seat of thought and the source of all intentions and ideas. The tongue then gave these thoughts form and reality through speech. Therefore, together, they became the tools of creation. To put it simply, the mighty Ptah thought about creating the world and spoke it into existence. Since this creation myth also coexisted with that of Heliopolis, some even claimed that it was Ptah who uttered the words that led to the creation of Atum.

Every god, river, star, and living being started as a thought in Ptah's heart. When he spoke, these thoughts emerged from the void of nothingness and began taking form and substance. Now that Ptah was no longer alone, as he was accompanied by the gods who had been born from his own words, the responsibilities to shape the world were split between them. Some became rulers, while others were caretakers of the various elements and aspects of the world.

Interestingly, in comparison to the Heliopolitan creation story, Ptah's version did not gain the same widespread acceptance among the majority of the ancient Egyptians. This was largely due to the fact that the Heliopolitan myth was bolstered by the political and religious influence of Heliopolis itself. The city was a religious and cultural center of the ancient Egyptians for a long time.

Hermopolitan Creation Myth

The last creation myth presents a rather unique perspective on the origin of the cosmos. The Hermopolitan narrative actually has a few different versions, each captivating in its own right.

The first version gave the spotlight to the Ogdoad, a group of eight deities, four males and their four female counterparts. These gods represented the fundamentals of chaos: water, darkness, infinity, and mystery. They were Nun and Naunet (representing the primeval waters), Amun and Amaunet (the water's hidden and mysterious nature), Huh and Hauhet (the water's infinity), and Kek and Kauket (darkness of the water). The Ogdoad as a whole was believed to have dwelled in the depths of Nun, the chaotic waters that existed before creation.

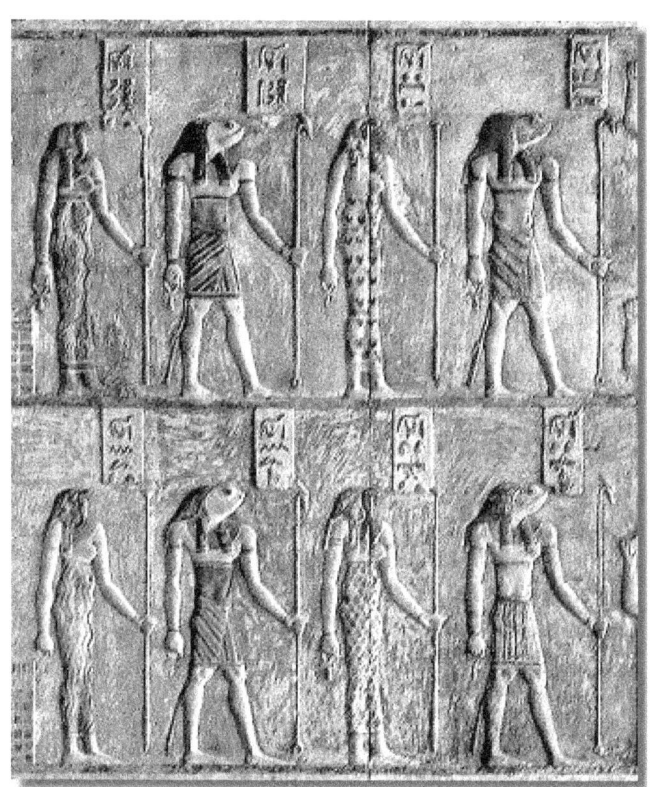

A depiction of the Ogdoad at the Hathor Temple in Dendera. The male deities were often depicted with frog heads, while their female counterparts had serpent heads.'

It was within this realm of chaos and nothingness that a mystical event occurred. From the interactions of these eight divine beings, a great mound emerged. Almost immediately, it broke the endless surface of the stagnant waters. This was the start of creation. It was also believed that these eight gods were the earliest to have ruled the earth. However, these primordial deities were not immortal. When their time had passed, the Ogdoad moved to the underworld, or the Du'at, where they resided for eternity.

Still, their task was far from over. From this new residence, the Ogdoad kept their eyes wide open, ensuring that the sun rose every day. As long as they were in power, the Ogdoad would make sure that the Nile continued to flow, ensuring the Egyptians could see the inundation visit their crops every year.

Meanwhile, there was also another version of the Hermopolitan creation story that spoke of how the world came from a cosmic egg. The egg itself was said to have been created either by the Ogdoad or laid by a long-forgotten celestial goose named the Gengen-Wer. From this divine egg came Ra, the mighty sun god, who then worked to create the world and everything else in it.

As the narratives evolved, the Ogdoad, which were initially central to the Hermopolitan myth, gradually faded from the official Egyptian pantheon, though their names remained in oral and written legends. Of course, their names were not entirely forgotten. Instead, they were overshadowed by the growing influence of other powerful deities, especially Ra. The falcon-headed sun god would be placed at the top of the pantheon, becoming chief of all Egyptian gods.

Narratives and legends in Egypt never stopped evolving, especially when the kingdom entered a new era. The New Kingdom period, for instance, saw the emergence of yet another creator deity. Known as Amun-Ra (the amalgamation of the god Amun and Ra), the deity was thought to be a self-created being and the ultimate originator of all that exists. He was often depicted as an invisible force or a hidden god whose power and presence permeated the entire universe itself. This narrative was accepted widely, especially at Karnak, the religious center of the kingdom at the time.

Another creation narrative that surfaced during this period involved the god named Khnum. Depicted with the head of a ram, the god was mainly worshiped on the island of Elephantine. According to this myth, Khnum used his divine potter's wheel to create the very first humans. In comparison to the other creation myths, this particular story emphasizes not how the earth and its elements came to be but rather the individuality of each human life and the careful attention of the divine in the creation process.

Chapter 2: The Sun and the Sky: Ra and Nut

The ancient Egyptians were exceptional farmers. Perhaps it was true that they were bestowed the sacred knowledge of agriculture by Osiris himself since they knew exactly how to make use of the resources and fertile lands that the gods had given them. The fertile banks of the Nile, in particular, were the greatest witness to the Egyptians' agricultural prowess. Rejuvenated by the river's annual flooding, these fields were often filled with an abundance of crops, especially wheat and barley—these two were the staples of their diet. Flax, which painted the Egyptian landscape in hues of subtle green, was also a popular crop. With its slender stems, the fiber of this crop was spun into fine linen. The ancient Egyptians also grew tall papyrus plants, which were then turned into papers and scrolls. This allowed them to record the civilization's greatest tales, feats, and history.

This abundance in agriculture did more than just feed the people. In fact, agriculture was the heart of the Egyptian economy. The kingdom thrived and was so wealthy in natural resources to the point that it eventually caught the attention of many other colossal powers at the time. The mighty Romans and the fierce Assyrians, for instance, were among the biggest rivals of the kingdom; they were aware that to control the fertile lands meant absolute wealth and power.

It is also clear that the ancient Egyptians were religious. Despite their busy schedules of toiling the land or sculpting statues of their pharaohs, they never failed to spare some time to look up at the sky and say their gratitude to the mighty sun. To them, the sun was not merely a burning star in the heavens. They viewed the sun with great reverence. After all, it was the sun that showed them when to plant and when to harvest. It was also the sun that had kept them alive and ensured their land was so fertile.

The ancient Egyptians were also very superstitious. Failing to respect and show their gratitude to certain elements of the divine would undoubtedly result in misfortune. The sun was no exception; disrespecting it could easily result in their lives being turned upside down. Drought could replace the inundation that nourished their crops, leaving them with nothing but starvation and catastrophe.

And so, they placed the god Ra on the highest throne of the Egyptian pantheon. He was the embodiment of the great sun itself, whose existence brought light, warmth, and growth. The Egyptians respected the divine being, especially since he was a constant companion in their journey through the seasons.

Ra was often depicted in many forms, each symbolizing his immense power. However, more often than not, Ra appeared on reliefs, texts, and sculptures as a man with the head of a falcon. On his head, he typically wore a sun disk encircled by a cobra, which signified his royal status and divine nature. This image of Ra could be seen etched on the walls of many temples and tombs in Egypt. The most significant site dedicated to the god was the Sun Temple at Heliopolis. Also known as one of the oldest cities in Egypt, Heliopolis was the center of Ra's veneration. Although the state of both the temple and the city is today only a shadow of its former glory, back then, it was undoubtedly a sight to behold. The temple complex once featured towering obelisks that pierced the sky, along with sets of colossal statues that stood as an homage to the mighty Ra. What is left for us today, unfortunately, is only ruins and dust.

Other than being carved onto walls of tombs and temples, Ra's image could also be

A depiction of Ra, the chief god of the Egyptian pantheon.[8]

found on an array of intricate artifacts like amulets, statuettes, and colorful paintings on the surface of a sarcophagus. These artifacts did not serve only as decoration. Most of them were used as talismans of protection; the ancient Egyptians would use them to invoke Ra's power against evil or chaos.

Jewelry featuring Ra adorned with the sun disk and holding the ankh.⁴

Being one of the superior gods in the Egyptian pantheon, it is not surprising that Ra features in multiple myths. The most popular one tells the story of an aging Ra. After he grew weary of ruling the earth for many centuries, Ra chose to ascend to the heavens. He did not hang his weapons once he got there; instead, Ra continued to reign from above.

Ra would embark on a grand voyage across the sky every day, from dawn until dusk. According to ancient texts, his solar vessel was known as the Mandjet, the "Boat of Millions of Years." It was described to be magnificent; it was made of gold and adorned with precious stone. His trip during the day was nearly free from obstacles. However, when twilight descended, the god's journey took a darker turn. This was also the time when Ra would transform into his alternative appearance: a man with the head of a ram. Aboard a different vessel known as the Mesektet Barque, Ra would plunge beyond the horizon and into the waters, eventually arriving in the bleak underworld.

Ra, in his ram-headed form, traveling through the underworld on the Mesektet Barque.[5]

The journey was far from being a simple walk in the park. In this realm, the sun god had to pass through twelve gates of the underworld, each leading to a different region. While some accounts suggest that the god took at least an hour to reach each gate, others claimed he took longer. During this part of the journey, Ra was said to have paid his respects to Osiris, the god of the underworld himself.

Ra was the chief god of the Egyptian pantheon, but this status alone did not guarantee his fate—and, by extension, the world's fate. The god had to be extra vigilant the entire time he was in the underworld, especially when he was a short distance away from reaching the exit. The nearer he got to the end of the underworld, the closer he was to meeting his greatest enemy of all time: Apophis.

Also known as Apep, this divine entity was a colossal serpent (sometimes depicted as a massive cobra) that represented darkness, chaos, and disorder. Its only task was to battle Ra as he passed through the underworld. The giant serpent wanted to devour the sun and plunge the world into eternal darkness where nothing could survive. Every night, Ra would fight fiercely against him. The sun god would win each night, and Apophis would slither back into hiding, preparing himself for yet another encounter with Ra the next day.

However, there were times when the battle took place slightly differently. Apophis would sometimes gain the upper hand and succeed in swallowing Ra. Without the sun god, the earth was thrown into darkness and uncertainty. Today, this event is recognized as a solar eclipse.

Of course, Ra could not be defeated permanently. Legend has it that whenever this happened, Ra had the help of other deities, particularly Set. It was said that despite Apophis's colossal size, he was incapable of holding Ra in his stomach for too long. The serpent would eventually regurgitate the sun god, allowing Ra to break free and emerge victorious each time. With the battle won, Ra would transform back into his falcon-headed form and board the Mandjet. He would then continue his journey across the sky, bringing forth light and warmth to the people once again. The first light of dawn was seen by the Egyptians as a sign that order had been restored and the cycle of day and night would continue.

Apophis or Apep based on a depiction in the tomb of pharaoh Ramesses I.[6]

As time passed, the Egyptians began to merge Ra with other deities, creating amalgamations that reflected the evolving religious and political landscape. By the time of the New Kingdom, the Egyptians saw the rising prominence of a god named Amun. Originally a local god of Thebes, Amun gained more and more worshipers over time, and his influence eventually rivaled that of Ra. By the 16th century BCE, the two gods had merged, becoming Amun-Ra, which became a symbol of unified divine power.

Amun-Ra seated on his throne.[7]

Some might mistakenly think that Amun-Ra was a different name for Ra. He was more than that, though, at least in the eyes of the ancient Egyptians. Amun-Ra was a complex divine being that represented both the invisible forces of creation (Amun) and the visible source of life (Ra). Even his depictions in temples and inscriptions appeared different compared to Ra. Most of the time, he was often pictured as a man wearing a crown with two tall plumes. Amun-Ra could also bear features of both deities at the same time. Since he was also associated with fertility, he could appear as a ram (rams were regarded as symbols of fertility, rebirth, and resurrection back then) with either curved horns or a sun disk on his head like Ra.

Ra's influence also extended to the pharaohs. To elevate their status, these Egyptian rulers would typically align themselves closely with the sun god. It was common for the pharaohs to see themselves as earthly embodiments of Ra. Pharaohs would often incorporate Ra's name into their own to further solidify their sacred association with the mighty god. Ramesses II (also known as Ramesses the Great) is a great example of this since his name means "Born of Ra."

Being one of the most celebrated pharaohs of ancient Egypt, it is not surprising that Ramesses II's name is familiar to many. Not only did he expand the borders of Egypt and lead his people into a period of stability, but the great pharaoh also left a lasting legacy in the realm of Egyptian architecture. The temple of Abu Simbel is one of the greatest examples of Egyptian architecture. Carved out of a mountainside, the temple features colossal statues of the pharaoh himself seated alongside Amun-Ra and Ptah.

The most remarkable feature of Abu Simbel, however, is its alignment with the sun. Twice a year, on February 22nd and October 22nd, the sun's rays penetrate the inner sanctum of the temple, illuminating the statues of Ramesses and Amun-Ra while leaving the statue of Ptah, the god of darkness, in shadow. This spectacular phenomenon is not just an architectural marvel. Many saw it as a representation of Ra's journey through the sky and the underworld.

Nut, the Egyptian Sky Goddess

Nut was often portrayed as a woman stretched over the earth god Geb, enveloping him and all his creatures in a protective embrace. Her body, a vast canopy adorned with stars, represented the night sky. This image of Nut arching over the earth was not just a representation of the sky; it was also a symbol of her all-encompassing protection and the eternal cycle of day and night. In some depictions, Nut took the form of a cow or a sow, signifying her role as the mother of the gods. This maternal aspect was a vital part of her identity, highlighting her nurturing nature and her role in giving birth to and protecting the celestial bodies.

The ladder, or Maqet, is another sacred symbol associated with Nut. It represented the stairway to heaven, which was believed to help the deceased reach the goddess's domain. It was believed to be used by Osiris to ascend into her heavenly domain. This symbol was often placed in tombs as a means of protection for the deceased, ensuring their safe passage into the afterlife under Nut's watchful gaze. Egyptian artists also portrayed Nut as a woman holding a pot of water, which represented her role as the giver of rain, essential for the fertility and sustenance of the earth.

Nut, arching over Geb, supported by the god of air, Shu.*

Pepi I Meryre, the third pharaoh of the Sixth Dynasty of Egypt, held Nut in such high regard. This deep reverence could be seen on the walls of his tomb chamber, which were heavily adorned with a collection of Pyramid Texts dedicated to the goddess. These texts included a hymn to Nut, which was more than just a set of verses. It was also a sacred invocation, a plea for protection, and a celebration of Nut's divine nature. The walls transformed the tomb into a sanctum of celestial magic, aligning the resting place of the pharaoh with the heavenly realm of Nut.

The integration of the hymn in Pepi I's tomb highlights the enduring influence of Nut in Egyptian religious practices, particularly concerning the afterlife. The pharaoh's association with Nut in his eternal resting place was believed to ensure his safe passage through the night sky and secure his rebirth in the afterlife.

Despite her important role in mythology and art, the worship of Nut was not as common as that of other Egyptian deities. Her presence was more ethereal, tied to the cosmos and the natural world rather than the more tangible aspects of daily life.

Nut's role in the cosmos was tied to her relationship with Ra, the sun god. As the sky goddess, she played a critical role in the cycle of the sun and, by extension, the cycle of life and death.

One of the most captivating myths involving Nut is her role in the sun's rebirth. Each evening, as Ra completed his journey across the sky, he would descend into Nut's embrace. She would then swallow him, marking the end of the day and the beginning of the night. In the depths of Nut's celestial body, Ra would travel through the night, undergoing a process of renewal and rebirth. Come dawn, Nut would give birth to Ra once again. He would be reborn and revitalized and begin his new journey across the sky.

Nut swallowing the sun, allowing it to travel through her body at night and be reborn at dawn.'

Nut's role in this process was very important. She was the guardian of the sun during the vulnerable hours of the night. She was the nurturer who ensured its rejuvenation and the birth-giver who brought forth the sun with the new day. However, Ra was not always on the same page as Nut. The two gods once had a major disagreement.

Nut was married to Geb, the god of earth, who was also her brother. They were said to be deeply in love. However, Ra did not bless their union. Some claim that the sun god was deeply enamored with Nut, while others suggested that Ra was fearful of a prophecy that a child of Nut would one day surpass him. Whatever the reason was, the sun god was said to have placed a curse upon Nut. He decreed that the sky goddess could not give birth to her children any day of the year. This curse was a devastating blow to Nut.

In her distress, Nut turned to Thoth, the god of wisdom and knowledge, for assistance. Thoth, known for his cleverness, devised a plan to outwit Ra's curse. He challenged Khonsu, the moon god, to a game of senet, a popular board game in ancient Egypt. Thoth was a master of the game and won several rounds, each time claiming a small portion of Khonsu's lunar light as his prize.

With the light he won, Thoth created five extra days, known as the "epagomenal days," which were not part of the regular Egyptian calendar year. This ingenious solution effectively circumvented Ra's curse since these days existed outside the bounds of the established year.

During these five magical days, Nut was able to give birth to her five children: Osiris, Horus the Elder (not to be confused with the falcon god of the same name), Set, Isis, and Nephthys. Each was born on a separate day. Osiris, born on the first of these days, grew up to become an important figure in Egyptian mythology. He is often associated with resurrection and the afterlife. Horus the Elder, Set, Isis, and Nephthys each played their own unique role in the pantheon.

News of the birth of these gods eventually reached Ra. Upon learning about the tricks that Nut and Thoth had pulled to evade his curse, the sun god flew into a rage. Fueled by anger and a sense of betrayal, Ra made a momentous decision that would forever alter the fabric of the cosmos and the fate of the two lovers, Nut and Geb.

Ra summoned Shu, the god of the air and wind, and gave him a daunting task. He ordered Shu to stand forever between Nut and Geb, ensuring that the sky and the earth would be separated. This decree forever changed the natural order and the lives of Nut and Geb.

Shu, bound by his duty to Ra, obeyed the command. He positioned himself beneath Nut, lifting her high above. Nut arched gracefully across the heavens and became the sky itself. Below her, Geb lay as the earth, sprawling and verdant, forever gazing up at his beloved yet never able to join her.

This separation of Nut and Geb explained the fundamental structure of the world. It was a powerful and poetic image as well: the sky and the earth, two eternal lovers, close yet forever apart.

Chapter 3: Chaos and Order: Set and Osiris

According to mythology, Osiris was Egypt's very first king. He was the first to unite Egypt and rule humankind. Osiris was so kind and fair that the ancient Egyptians held him in high regard. He was praised for his wisdom, justice, and nurturing spirit. Under his benevolent reign, the people knew no chaos. War was not common, and it seemed as if peace would be everlasting. The Nile's waters never failed to flood the fields, allowing the granaries of Egypt to be overflowed with bountiful harvests. Osiris was also believed to have been the one to have taught humans the art of agriculture and civilization. These precious contributions made him the most adored king of Egypt; he was revered as not merely a ruler but also a divine guardian.

But, of course, not everyone looked up to him. Set, in particular, was jealous of his brother, Osiris. The god of chaos was often associated with the wild desert winds and storms. He was equally revered and feared for the chaos he represented. Despite not being abandoned by the Egyptians (they also worshiped Set back then, as he embodied balance), Set wanted more. The god of chaos could not sit still while his brother continued to sit on the throne, bringing harmony and order to the world. He wished to sit on the throne himself so he could impose his own rule of unpredictability and strife.

To make his ambitions come true, Set devised a rather sinister plan to usurp the throne. He began crafting a chest that was so exquisite that it would tempt anyone who laid eyes upon it. It was made with only the best materials, including rare pieces of wood, gold, and precious stones. This masterpiece of craftsmanship was not meant to be a gift for his brother. It was specifically designed to ensnare Osiris.

The god of chaos organized a lavish banquet. He invited nearly the entire pantheon of gods and goddesses, along with several foreign monarchs. It was an unimaginable feast with plenty of food and beautiful decorations. Among the guests was none other than Osiris, who was oblivious to his brother's scheme. Without wasting too much time, Set brought out the beautiful wooden chest. Perhaps with a sinister smile on his face, the god of chaos proclaimed that the chest would be gifted to whomever it fit perfectly. Little did the guests know, but Set had already constructed the chest to fit only Osiris. One by one, the guests tried to fit into the chest, and no one succeeded in doing so.

Finally, it was Osiris's turn to lay down in the chest. He fit into it like a glove. This was the very moment Set had been waiting for. He sprang into action, closing the lid and sealing the chest shut. Some suggest that this was the precursor of Egyptian sarcophagi. Set's plan did not end there. He immediately took the chest containing his brother and cast it into the Nile.

The chest—or perhaps the coffin—was swept away for many days. It drifted along the Nile and finally out to sea, where it eventually reached the shores near Byblos. The coffin was left untouched, and as time passed, a great tamarisk tree grew around it as if it were protecting the chest and the remains of the mighty god inside it.

Since the tamarisk had a powerful god within it, the tree gave out a divine aura, attracting those who passed by. One of them was the king of Byblos. Perhaps sensing magic or a sense of divinity in the great tamarisk, the king ordered the tree to be cut down. He then commanded that its trunk (the part that contained Egypt's most revered god and king) be brought straight to his grand palace so that he could use it as a pillar to support the roof of his house.

With Osiris gone, the throne was vacant. Knowing that there was no obstacle in his way, Set proclaimed himself the new king of Egypt. His reign was a stark contrast to the golden era of Osiris. The kingdom had enjoyed prosperity. However, with Set wearing the crown, crops withered, and the people despaired. It was as if the desert expanded its reach. Violent storms broke out, sweeping through the kingdom and leaving destruction in its wake. Agriculture became a thing of the past with the absence of the river's annual inundation.

It is important to note that the tale of Set and Osiris is not merely a story of envy and betrayal. It is a narrative that reflects the timeless dance of opposing forces and a reminder of the eternal struggle that lies at the heart of existence. Although Set was often pictured as an antagonist, especially in the story of Osiris, the god actually held a more complex and nuanced role. Despite his association with chaos, storms, and the desert, Set was an essential figure in the pantheon since he played a crucial role in maintaining the balance of the universe.

Many thousands of years ago, Set was placed on the higher levels of the pantheon. He was revered by the Egyptians as one of the most powerful deities to exist. His worship could be seen especially prominent in Upper Egypt, particularly in the city of Naqada. His reverence lasted for centuries; Ramesses II, for instance, held the god of chaos in high regard. He was also seen as a patron of warriors due to his strength and fierceness. Pharaohs often invoked Set's power in warfare, seeking his aid in battles.

Set holding the ankh and the Was scepter.[10]

Rituals and ceremonies dedicated to Set were known for their intensity. Some agree that this reflected his forceful nature. These rituals often involved animal sacrifices, which were seen as a way to appease and honor the god. However, not all animals could be sacrificed in the name of Set. Most of the time, the Egyptians would choose creatures that were associated with the god, such as pigs, donkeys, or hippopotami.

Temples dedicated to Set were once common, although they were not widespread in every city. The greatest example is the Temple of Set at Naqada. Unfortunately, much of this temple has been claimed by Mother Nature. However, many artifacts depicting Set, including statues and reliefs, have been unearthed in various archaeological sites across Egypt. These artifacts often portray Set in his animal form.

One of the most intriguing aspects of Set's representation in Egyptian art is the Set animal (sometimes known as the sha). This creature has a slender body and a squared head with a long snout. To untrained eyes, the creature may appear similar to a dog. However, these features are not attributable to any known animal, which clearly signifies the mysterious and unique nature of the god Set.

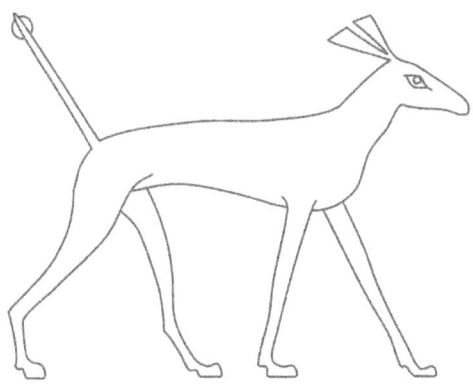

A drawing of the Set animal or sha.[11]

In the eyes of the ancient Greeks, Set's mysterious and formidable character found a parallel in their own mythology. They identified Set with Typhon, a monstrous serpentine giant and one of the deadliest creatures in Greek mythology.

In Greek mythology, Typhon was known as the father of all monsters. He was a fearsome figure of destruction and chaos. He was said to have the power to spew fire and challenge the might of Zeus, the king of the Greek gods. This image of Typhon is very similar to Set, who, in Egyptian mythology, was often seen as a figure of disruption and disorder. Both deities embodied the raw forces of nature and the untamed aspects of the world. Just as Typhon was essential in the Greek pantheon despite his fearsome nature, Set played a crucial role in Egyptian myths. The only difference, however, is that Typhon was a monstrous figure and never a symbol of balance. Set, on the other hand, had a crucial role in maintaining the balance of Ma'at (the Egyptian concept of balance and order) despite being seen as an adversary to gods like Osiris and Horus.

Apart from being highlighted as the main antagonist in the tale of Osiris, Set also starred in an episode involving Ra's fight against Apophis. Interestingly, Set was not associated with Ra at all initially. He was primarily associated with chaos, deserts, storms, and foreign lands.

However, over time, as Egyptian religious beliefs evolved, Set's role in the mythology underwent significant changes. This shift is partly attributed to the political and social changes in Egypt, where a god's role was often reinterpreted to reflect the changing dynamics of power and beliefs.

The turning point for Set's role came during the Second Intermediate Period of Egypt. Historically, this was a time of great turmoil and foreign invasions. Set was associated with foreign lands, so he was initially viewed in a negative light. However, once the Egyptians successfully repelled these invasions, Set began to be seen more as a defender against external chaos rather than a bringer of it. This reimagining of Set's role paved the way for his portrayal as a protector.

And so, a myth that pictured Set as a mighty protector emerged. In this story, he could be seen defending Ra aboard the sun god's barque. Set was thought to have possessed formidable strength and ferocity, and many Egyptians held on to the belief that he was one of the few gods who could stand against Apophis. He was often depicted standing at the prow of Ra's boat, fiercely fighting off the serpent with his spear. Some sources claim there were times when Apophis successfully hypnotized Ra and the other gods present on the barque. Only Set managed to resist the cobra's magic, allowing him to defeat Apophis with his divine spear. This role highlights a more positive aspect of Set's character. By protecting Ra, Set ensured the continuation of the cycle of day and night, which was crucial for life on Earth and in the underworld.

Set thrusting his spear into Apophis, ensuring Ra's protection.[19]

Osiris, a God Revered in Both Life and Death

Following the success of Set's brutal scheme, Osiris was left with no choice but to go through a fate worse than death. Not only was he torn from the throne of Egypt, but he was also trapped inside the chest for a very long time. Eventually, he suffocated and died. Yet, his journey was far from being over. His remains would not stay in the grand palace of the Byblos king forever. Isis, Osiris's loyal wife, although in mourning, would embark on a quest to find and resurrect her beloved husband—a tale we will explore in more detail later on.

Ultimately, Isis succeeded in retrieving Osiris and resurrected him. However, fate had already been written; the living world had to bid farewell to Osiris. To follow his destiny, Osiris had to resign from his title as the beloved king of Egypt and transition to become the god of the underworld. True, his absence was felt in the world of the living, but the realm of the dead saw the arrival of a just and wise king who would remain there for eternity, adjudicating over the souls of the departed.

Wall painting in the tomb of Pharaoh Horemheb featuring Osiris (seated), Anubis, and Horus.[18]

In his new role, Osiris acted as a steward to the souls of the deceased. Because of his association with the underworld, he was often depicted as a mummified king. His skin was green, which represented vegetation and rebirth, while his pharaoh's beard was associated with royalty. He was also often depicted with a crook and a flail crossed over his chest. The crook signified kingship, guidance, and protection, similar to a shepherd's care for his flock, and the flail represented authority, discipline, and fertility.

The mythology surrounding Osiris influenced Egyptian burial practices. His story encouraged the belief in an afterlife, a realm where justice and harmony prevailed under his wise rule, which led to the development of elaborate burial rituals, with the deceased being equipped with spells and items necessary for a safe journey to the afterlife. The Book of the Dead, a collection of spells and instructions, was often placed in tombs to guide the deceased through the Duat (the Egyptian underworld) and into the presence of Osiris.

Osiris was revered as the original archetype of kingship. The pharaohs of Egypt were seen as earthly embodiments of Horus, the falcon-headed god and son of Osiris. However, upon their death, the pharaoh's association transitioned from Horus to Osiris. In death, they were believed to have become Osiris himself. This belief was central to Egyptian funerary practices, as the mummification process and burial rituals were designed to mirror what Osiris went through. The pharaohs were mummified to resemble the god with the intention of being reborn in the afterlife, just as Osiris was resurrected by Isis.

A depiction of Osiris judging the dead in the Hall of Judgment from the Book of the Dead.[14]

The worship of Osiris was widespread. His cult centers could be seen dotted throughout Egypt. The most significant of these was Abydos, where the Osireion, a large temple complex dedicated to him, became a major pilgrimage site. Here, the faithful gathered to celebrate the mysteries of Osiris, rituals that commemorated his death and resurrection. Another important cult center was at Busiris in the Nile Delta. Here, he was worshiped as the lord of the underworld and the judge of the dead.

It is not surprising that Osiris's influence extended beyond religious practices. He became an important part of the daily lives of ancient Egyptians. When he was alive, Osiris was seen as a just and benevolent ruler. He was considered an ideal king who had brought civilization to Egypt. His death and resurrection, on the other hand, were seen as the ultimate acts of sacrifice for the benefit of all mankind. This narrative of a god-king who triumphs over betrayal and death resonated deeply with the Egyptian people, offering them hope and comfort in the face of their own mortality.

His relationship with other deities, especially his wife Isis and his son Horus, further enriched the mythology surrounding him. Isis's devotion to resurrect Osiris and Horus's quest to avenge his father's death showed the importance of familial loyalty and divine justice.

Osiris (middle) flanked by his son, Horus (left), and his wife, Isis (right).[15]

Osiris was honored in many festivals and celebrations. The most popular of all was the Khoiak festival. During this festival, the ancient Egyptians would engage in a series of rituals that culminated in the planting of "Osiris beds," which were filled with soil and barley. This was to symbolize the resurrection of life from the dead earth. Scholars suggest that this ritualistic planting was a physical manifestation of the Egyptians' deep connection with agriculture and their belief in the cyclical nature of life, death, and rebirth, as personified by Osiris.

Chapter 4: Love and Magic: Isis

In 51 BCE, Cleopatra rose to the throne of Egypt. She was of Macedonian origins, yet the queen succeeded in gaining the favor of the majority of her subjects. Cleopatra was the only Ptolemaic pharaoh who could speak Egyptian despite her veins not carrying any Egyptian blood. Interestingly, Egyptian and Greek were not the only languages she was fluent in; Cleopatra could speak at least nine different languages. Perhaps this fluency in different tongues was one of the factors that contributed to her diplomatic prowess.

As a pharaoh, Cleopatra knew she had to appear extravagant. It was common for her to appear in public dressed in a kalasiris. This simple yet elegant sheath dress was a staple of Egyptian fashion at that time. Cleopatra was also said to have worn exquisite jewelry and precious stones. On her head, she would have sported a diadem. However, it was during religious ceremonies that Cleopatra's image caught the attention of many.

Typically, during these sacred occasions, the pharaoh would transform her image into that of the goddess Isis. She would wear a different kind of sheath dress that was likely more extravagant than usual. It is plausible that her ceremonial dresses were made of fine, pleated linen. They were also dyed in colors that symbolized divinity and royalty. Over her dress, the queen might have worn the Usekh, a type of collar or necklace usually worn only by Egyptian royals and elites. Even their goddesses were often depicted wearing one. Her other jewelry included bracelets and anklets, each bearing motifs associated with Isis, such as the scarab, lotus flower, or the sun disk cradled between the horns of a cow. The latter represented another goddess, Hathor, who was closely linked to Isis.

The vulture crown.[16]

Instead of a simple diadem, Cleopatra wore ceremonial headgear, such as the vulture crown. Just as the name suggests, the crown was in the shape of a vulture, with both of its wings hanging down on both sides. Apart from its unique shape, the crown also featured hundreds of gemstones, from lapis lazuli to turquoise. Other sources also suggest that the queen once appeared before her subjects wearing a headdress resembling a throne or a seat, a symbol of the goddess Isis and royalty. According to tradition, Isis was a personification of the throne.

To the ancient Egyptians, Cleopatra was more than just a ruler. She was thought to be the living manifestation of Isis, who was the goddess of motherhood, magic, and healing. The queen herself embraced this view. She knew it was important to align herself with the core values of Egyptian society, which included devotion, loyalty, and the sanctity of family.

So, what role did Isis exactly play in Egyptian mythology, and why was the goddess held in such high regard, especially by women? The answer is simple: Isis was considered the divine mother of the pharaoh. Also known in Egyptian as Aset or Eset, Isis was one of the most important beings in the Heliopolitan creation myth. She was one of the offspring of Geb (the god of the earth) and Nut (the sky goddess). Her siblings were Osiris, Set, and Nephthys. With Osiris, who was also her husband, the two had a child named Horus (the falcon-headed god), who later became the divine model of kingship itself.

Isis as depicted in the tomb of Seti I, 1360 BCE.[17]

As a goddess of magic, she was believed to possess profound and secret knowledge, giving her power over all beings. Her power even surpassed that of Ra, the chief god. Her magical abilities were most famously depicted in the story of Osiris's resurrection, where she used her powers to reassemble his body and bring him back to life.

Isis was also known as the goddess of magic. She was said to have possessed all knowledge in the universe, giving her power over all beings. Her power surpassed even that of Ra, the god of the sun. Her magical abilities could be seen clearly in the story of Osiris's resurrection. Isis was also revered as the goddess of motherhood and fertility. Her devotion to Osiris and Horus is still remembered as the ideal of maternal love and dedication. Being a healer, ancient Egyptians often invoked her name for protection and the healing of illnesses.

Similar to other important deities of the Egyptian pantheon, like Ra, Osiris, and Horus, Isis had many temples built in her honor. The most significant of all was the Philae Temple Complex. Currently located on Agilkia Island near Aswan (the temple complex was initially built on Philae Island until it was relocated in the 20th century CE due to a flood). This temple was also the center of her cult. Complete with grand pylons and awe-inspiring colonnades, the temple complex impressed many with its towering gateways and intricate reliefs depicting scenes of the goddess and her divine family. Inside the temple were more hieroglyphs that told the stories of her myths and her strong love for Osiris. One could also find a sanctuary located at the center of the temple. This sacred room was where a statue of Isis was kept. Most of the time, this room was dimly lit. Religious ceremonies once took place there. Ancient Egyptians would flock to the temple to make offerings and pray to receive the goddess's blessings.

Temple of Isis in Philae, Aswan, Egypt.[18]

Isis's influence was not only limited to Egypt. The goddess also found a place within Roman culture and religion. Initially, the worship of Isis was viewed with skepticism in the Eternal City. This was mostly due to its foreign origins. However, as time passed, the cult of Isis gained popularity, especially among the commoners. Many were attracted to Isis because of the universal themes in her stories. The stories of resurrection, healing, and protection resonated deeply with the Roman populace. Eventually, the Eternal City accepted her worship more openly to the point where festivals were held in honor of the goddess. One of them was known as the Navigium Isidis, which celebrated the start of the sailing season.

It is safe to assume that the integration of Isis into Roman culture had to do with Cleopatra, who had significant influence over the Romans after her relationships with Julius Caesar and Mark Antony. Temples and statues of Isis began to dot Roman cities. The Romans were known for assimilating deities from other cultures, so it is not a surprise that Isis was woven into their religious beliefs. Her image, however, went through some changes; this modification was done to align her more with Roman sensibilities. In the Eternal City, it was more common to see her depicted in Roman garb and have attributes that made her more relatable to the Roman populace.

Later on, Isis became closely associated with Venus (Aphrodite in Greek mythology), who was known as the Roman goddess of love and beauty. This association largely stemmed from the similar attributes both deities shared, such as femininity, motherhood, and a strong connection to nature and fertility. Both goddesses were also seen as patrons of sailors and protectors of the seas.

However, it is important to note that while there were similarities, Isis and Aphrodite/Venus remained distinct entities within their respective mythologies. Isis's role within the Egyptian pantheon was deeply rooted in themes of magic, resurrection, and familial devotion, which were not primary attributes of Aphrodite/Venus. Nonetheless, the blending of these goddesses in the Roman period highlights the cultural exchanges and religious syncretism that occurred in the ancient world.

The Legend of How Isis Tricked the Sun God, Ra

According to legend, Isis sought to gain the same power as Ra, the mightiest god of the Egyptian pantheon. True, Ra was wise and powerful, but his old age was slowly catching up to him. Legend has it that the sun god was beginning to weaken--though not entirely. His saliva was said to have dribbled as he spoke, and he no longer had the same control over the vast world as he had in his prime. This was the very opportunity that Isis was patiently waiting for.

The goddess aimed not to seize power from the sun god but rather to expand her abilities. She knew that Ra's power was in his secret name, a name that held the essence of his true being and the source of his divine power. However, this name was a closely guarded secret known only to Ra himself. Determined to learn this name, Isis devised a plan. She collected the saliva that dribbled from Ra's mouth as he slept and mixed it with earth, creating a venomous snake.

This snake was then placed on Ra's path. When Ra walked by, the snake bit him, injecting its potent venom. The pain was immediate and intense, but no god or magician could relieve Ra's suffering since the poison was of divine creation.

In her guise as a healer, Isis approached Ra. She offered to cure him but only on the condition that he reveal his secret name to her. Ra was in unbearable agony, but he resisted at first, offering her wealth and power instead, but none of these could sway Isis. She knew that only his secret name would give her the power she desired.

Eventually, weakened by pain and realizing he had no other option, Ra consented. He whispered his secret name to Isis, which granted her an immense power that rivaled his own. With this knowledge, Isis healed Ra of the snake's venom, but from that moment forward, she held a portion of his power, elevating her status among the gods.

Divine Family Drama

When news of her husband's sudden death reached her, Isis was immediately overwhelmed with grief and sadness. Yes, her heart ached because she had lost her husband, but she was also in deep sorrow knowing that the world had been plunged into chaos and turmoil under Set. Isis could not sit and do nothing while her brother, Set, ruled over Egypt. The goddess knew she had to do everything she could to restore balance, and the first step to achieving that was to find Osiris's body.

The search was undeniably hard. Isis scoured Egypt day and night. After days, maybe weeks or months, of relentless searching, Isis's efforts were rewarded. She met a few children who saw a peculiar wooden chest floating in the direction of Byblos. And so, disguised as an old woman, Isis made her way to the city. The story says that the goddess managed to impress the queen of Byblos so much that she eventually entrusted the disguised Isis with the care of her son.

However, instead of nursing the Byblos prince as one normally would, Isis performed a secret ritual every night. She bathed the young prince in fire, which eventually purged him of his mortal constraints. While doing this, Isis was also said to have transformed into a swallow, flying around the palace in search of the pillar that held her husband. Eventually, the queen of Byblos stumbled upon the scene, flames dancing around the young prince. Horrified by the sight of her own son hugged by burning fire, the queen screamed as loud as she could. Perhaps startled by the scream and not wanting to cause further commotion, Isis quickly reverted to her true form. Revealing herself as a goddess and seizing the opportunity, Isis told her story and begged for the pillar that contained Osiris.

It was hard to deny a god, especially one that was well respected. With the pillar now in her possession, Isis carefully extracted the chest. After opening it, the goddess burst into tears. Her husband was lying still, his body cold. Knowing the danger that lingered if Set ever knew of her discovery, Isis hid the body in a marshland. She planned to perform the rituals that could resurrect Osiris.

Unfortunately for her, Set discovered Isis's actions. Overwhelmed with rage, Set was believed to have cut Osiris's body into fourteen pieces before scattering them all over Egypt. This act of desecration was a severe blow to Isis's hopes, but her resolve did not waver. The following morning, finding Osiris's body gone, Isis went on another journey. Thankfully, she was not alone in this quest. Nephthys, the wife of Set, helped out in the search effort and greatly aided Isis. Nephthys was, after all, a protector of the dead. She symbolized the death experience, just as Isis represented the experience of birth. So, together, the two goddesses combined their powers and wisdom in their quest to restore balance.

The task was daunting, but Isis was never known to back down. She eventually found the first piece of her dismembered husband, followed by the second, the third, and so on. With each discovery, Isis's determination grew. She eventually succeeded in retrieving all the pieces of her husband except for one, his penis, which had been eaten by a type of fish known as Oxyrhynchus (also known as Medjed). This was the reason why ancient Egyptians were prohibited from eating this fish.

With the thirteen pieces of Osiris gathered in one place, Isis and a few other gods, including Nephthys, Thoth, and Anubis, then began the task of reassembling —or sewing—Osiris's remains. Night after night, they worked, and when the body was whole again, they wrapped it in linen, creating the first mummy. Isis then worked on her magic. Only when the sky turned dark could the goddess resurrect Osiris and embrace him once more. It was believed that this was also the time that the two conceived their son, Horus.

Unfortunately, this act of resurrection was not able to hold Osiris in the living world for too long. The god embraced Isis once more and expressed his gratitude for her loyalty. However, he also told her that it was not his destiny to live in the same world as hers. Without all fourteen pieces of himself, Osiris was not allowed to live in the mortal realm. He was not to rule the living; instead, he would become the king of the afterlife. He was meant to remain in the Du'at (the world of the dead), where his main responsibility was to judge the souls of the departed.

Isis was clearly devastated. Osiris calmed his wife and reassured her that their legacy was not over yet. Osiris told her of a prophecy that would bring honor back to their family. Osiris claimed that their son, Horus, would defeat Set and rise as the great protector of the Egyptians. Horus would be the one to avenge Osiris, restore order, and reintroduce peace once more to Egypt after claiming the throne from Set. Isis was relieved by this, and she began accepting the fact that her husband had to move on.

Osiris's departure to the Du'at marked the beginning of his transition from a god and king of the living to the lord of the underworld. Isis, on the other hand, turned her focus on raising and protecting their son,

Horus. Yet, some claimed the goddess never stopped missing her husband. She would cry every year, her tears turning into the annual flood that took place across Egypt. However, despite missing her husband, Isis never failed to ensure her son's safety. The goddess was well aware that she must do everything in her power to ensure Horus's rightful place in the world. She had to keep her eyes open all the time since Horus's path was always filled with danger. His uncle, Set, knew no rest; he posed a constant threat to both Horus and Isis. Isis used her wisdom and magical skills to protect Horus until he was finally ready to challenge Set and reclaim the crown.

Isis and the Status of Women in Ancient Egypt

Isis was a major goddess in Egyptian mythology. She had a strong influence on the status and role of women in ancient Egypt. She was often portrayed as a devoted wife, a loving mother, and a powerful goddess—all qualities that gave women a positive role model to look up to.

In contrast to women from other ancient civilizations, women in ancient Egypt enjoyed more rights and higher status. Not only could they own property and run businesses, but Egyptian women were allowed to initiate divorce. The respect people had for Isis might have helped women gain more respect in everyday life.

The worship of Isis also provided women with a divine role model. Women were given a chance to devote themselves fully to the heavens. Some served as priestesses in temples built in honor of the goddess. They were also in charge of performing rituals and ceremonies. This way, women in Egypt were given a position of respect within their communities. Although the influence of Isis spread into the Roman world, her worship did not change the status of Roman women; the structure of Roman society remained mostly the same.

Beyond the ancient world, the legacy of Isis continues to resonate with people, finding relevance and undergoing reinterpretation in the modern era, notably within contemporary feminist discourse. In feminist perspectives, Isis is often viewed as an early embodiment of the empowered woman. Her narrative, characterized by resilience, intelligence, and the ability to protect and advocate for her family, parallels modern ideas about female empowerment and self-determination. The story of Isis—her journey to reclaim Osiris's body and her instrumental role in securing Horus's future—mirrors contemporary narratives where women actively shape their destiny and advocate for themselves and their loved ones. The influence of Isis also permeates modern culture, as she is often revisited in literature, art, and media. She is typically portrayed as a figure of wisdom, nurturing, and protection, underscoring her lasting impact across different cultures and time periods. Although no longer worshiped, the enduring legacy of Isis in the modern world serves as a source of inspiration and reflection in discussions about femininity, power, and resilience.

Chapter 5: The God of Mummification: Anubis

In ancient Egypt, belief in the afterlife reigned supreme. The art of mummification was more than just a mere ritual; it was seen as a bridge to eternity. The embalmer stood in a chamber filled with the aroma of incense and the weight of tradition. Surrounded by an array of tools forged from the finest bronze and iron, he prepared to embark on the meticulous journey of preservation. Under the watchful eyes of painted deities, the embalmer surveyed the room around him. The chamber was lined with jars of oils and spices, and in the center of the room lay the body. Before him was a variety of sharp flint knives, each serving its own unique purpose in the ritual. The deceased was a nobleman adorned in lavish garments, though they had to be removed. The embalmer began his work with ceremonial prayers, seeking the protection of the gods before he made the first incision. Once he finished praying to the gods, the embalmer made a small yet precise cut in the lower left abdomen.

He was not alone in this process. The embalmer was also accompanied by his assistants, who observed his delicate hands working on the operation. To ensure the mummification process went smoothly, he had to remove each organ inside the body. However, these organs were not to be discarded; each of them held its own significance. The first to be extracted was the intestines. This particular organ was believed to be the seat of turmoil. Therefore, it needed special attention. If left unattended or decayed, the soul of the deceased would face unrest in the afterlife.

Once successfully extracted in one piece, the intestines were carefully dropped into a large pottery bowl. Then, the bowl was filled with natron. This special type of preservative agent was found only in the dry lake beds to the northwest of Thebes. Natron was essential in the process of mummification; without it, the embalmer would not be able to prevent decomposition.

After the intestines, the embalmer moved on to remove the stomach, liver, and lungs. These organs were also treated gently. They were first cleaned before going through the process of preservation. The liver was a symbol of strength and vitality, but there is no clear evidence in surviving Egyptian texts that explains what specific symbolic meanings the other two organs held.

Only the heart was left inside the body, as this organ was said to have been the center of a person's being. According to traditional Egyptian beliefs, the heart encompassed a person's physical essence, thoughts, and feelings. It was highly important to keep it intact during the mummification process. However, ensuring the heart remained unscathed was not an easy task, even for the most experienced embalmer. The heart was located close to the lungs, so there was always the possibility of the embalmer accidentally hurting the organ as he removed the lungs.

It was only when the upper torso was emptied of its internal organs that the embalmer would move on to the next step. Using palm wine, he would clean the cavities, ensuring no blood could be seen and that no foul scent lingered in the air.

He then turned his attention back to the organs that he had carefully extracted. They were wrapped in linen and placed safely in canopic jars. These jars were not merely containers. Each was carved out of limestone and adorned with intricate hieroglyphs. These vessels were then closed off using different lids bearing the faces of the four sons of Horus. The stomach was sealed with a lid bearing an image of the jackal-headed god Duamutef, and the lungs were guarded by Hapi, which was depicted with the head of a baboon. Imsety, who had a human head, watched over the liver, and Qebehsenuef, with the head of a falcon, kept the intestines safe. These guardians ensured that the organs would be reunited with the body in the afterlife.

Animal-headed canopic jars from the Twenty-sixth Dynasty (664–525 BCE).[19]

The brain was considered by ancient Egyptians to be inconsequential. The embalmer would use a long, slender iron, which he carefully inserted through the nostrils. He would gently shove it in until he could feel the soft, delicate brain tissue. With skilled twists and turns, he fragmented the brain, with his assistant holding the head steady during the entire process. It is safe to assume that this task required both precision and patience. After multiple gentle prods, the brain would eventually turn into a thick, viscous liquid. Then, the embalmer and his assistants flipped the corpse over. They would slap the back of the skull, allowing the liquid to flow out through the dead person's nasal passage. Once the skull was free from even the tiniest bits of the brain, the embalmer would then meticulously clean the cranial cavity and prepare the skull for its eternal rest.

With the organs and brain finally removed, the body was now ready for desiccation. Again, natron, a naturally occurring salt, was the embalmer's main tool in this stage. The body was thoroughly cleaned and then covered inside and out with heaps of natron. The corpse, now seen as a vessel for the soul's journey, was left in a state of rest, completely submerged in natron. This period of desiccation lasted for forty days, during which the body slowly transformed. The natron absorbed all moisture, leaving the skin dry and leathery, leaving it perfectly preserved for the next stage.

After the natron treatment, the body was carefully unwrapped from its salty cocoon. It was cleansed once more, this time with oils and fragrances, in preparation for its final adornment. The wrapping of the body was considered a sacred act, so it was common for rituals and prayers to be performed. Then, the embalmer began to enfold the body in hundreds of yards of linen. As the layers of linen accumulated, the embalmer recited prayers. He believed each wrap was a step closer to immortality. Amulets and charms were also placed between the folds, ensuring protection and guidance in the underworld.

Once that was done, the embalmer placed a mask over the wrapped head of the mummy. The design and quality of these masks differed based on the deceased's social standing. Wealthy individuals often had elaborate masks adorned with gold and detailed with fine paint. Those from less affluent backgrounds typically had simpler masks featuring more basic designs without elaborate decorations. The situation was similar with amulets. The wealthy were buried with numerous amulets crafted from precious stones, while those with fewer resources might have only a handful of amulets made from less expensive materials.

A mummy mask.[30]

The process of mummification took a total of seventy days to complete. Only then would the mummy be prepared for its burial in a tomb, which had been designed and constructed in advance. These burials were typically accompanied by elaborate rituals intended to prepare the deceased for their journey into the next life. Mummies were often placed inside a sarcophagus, which was then placed in the burial chamber of the tomb. Once everything was in place, the entrance to the tomb was sealed, marking the moment when the soul of the departed began its journey to the afterlife.

Of course, such elaborate mummification was not done on everyone. Interestingly, recent studies found that there were no standardized methods of mummification across all the regions of Egypt. The less wealthy, for instance, were possibly mummified with simpler methods. More often than not, their organs were not removed. Instead, embalmers would pour juniper oil into the body cavity to dissolve the organs. Their bodies were also not wrapped intricately in linen but rather buried in the hot desert, which naturally dried them out and eventually preserved them.

Anubis, the Guide of the Dead

With the mummy securely placed within the sarcophagus and the tomb's entrance sealed, a profound transformation occurred. With the physical rites completed, the soul of the departed embarked on its journey into the realm of the afterlife.

In this realm of shadows, the deceased would be greeted by Anubis, the jackal-headed god. Although his role in ancient Egyptian mythology, especially in death and funerary rites, was important, Anubis had a rather inconsistent origin. Some sources claim Anubis was the son of Ra and was crowned as the god of the dead. In this early depiction, he was seen as the sole ruler of the afterlife. His connection to Ra further added a celestial aspect to his dominion, intertwining the cycles of life and death with the daily journey of the sun across the sky.

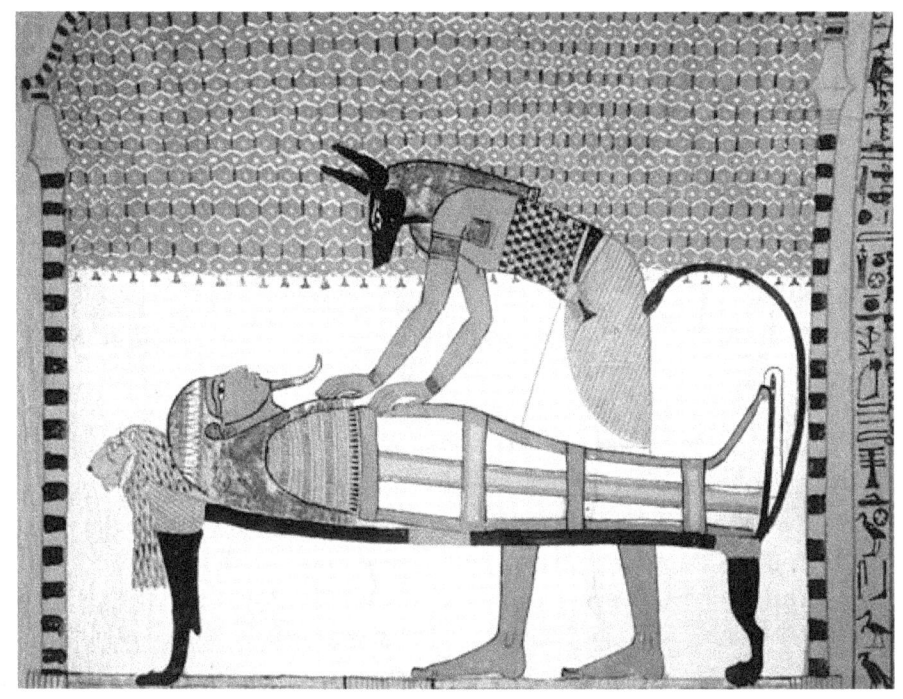

Anubis tending to a mummy.[31]

However, with the rise of Osiris's cult, this version of the story where Anubis was seen as the sole ruler of the underworld underwent a significant shift. The title of the king of the underworld was given to Osiris instead. Therefore, Anubis was no longer considered the primary ruler of the deceased. His role evolved, and he became known as the god of funerary rites and the guardian of the dead. Anubis became more closely related to the process of mummification and the protection of graves and cemeteries.

Then, by 2000 BCE, another origin story emerged that linked Anubis to Nephthys. Nephthys, who was married to Set, found herself drawn to Osiris. Perhaps driven by both lust and longing, Nephthys was said to have disguised herself as the goddess Isis and seduced Osiris. Through this union, Anubis was born. However, Nephthys was well aware of the wrath and retribution that would dawn upon her should Set ever discover her affair with Osiris. So, the goddess chose to make a heart-wrenching decision. She left the newborn Anubis in a desolate area, abandoning him so that she could conceal evidence of her infidelity. Set eventually discovered this affair, which further fueled his desire to end Osiris.

As for Anubis, Isis discovered him. The goddess knew of the affair between Osiris and Nephthys, but as the goddess of motherhood and compassion, she did not have the heart to abandon Anubis. She took the infant into her care, raising him as her own. By doing so, she forged a bond of deep loyalty and gratitude in him. Perhaps as a gesture of gratitude, Anubis became her most loyal ally and supporter. This relationship was most prominently displayed in the myth of Osiris's resurrection.

His mysterious origins aside, we can safely assume that Anubis offered the dead solace in their journey through the afterlife. In Egyptian mythology, he was revered for his strength, wisdom, fairness, and knowledge of the mystical arts. He stood as the sentinel of the afterlife and a protector of the dead, guiding them through their journey to eternity.

The ancient Egyptian Book of the Dead was a sacred text that served as a guide, offering spells, prayers, and instructions to the deceased. The soul, accompanied by Anubis, embarked on a perilous path through this mystical domain, facing challenges that tested its worthiness for the afterlife.

This journey involved traversing through dark waters, confronting fearsome creatures, and navigating through gates guarded by formidable beings. Each step of the way, the soul encountered various gods and demons who presented their own riddles and tasks. These trials were essential since they purified the soul and prepared it for the ultimate judgment.

Anubis provided guidance and protection. He was the beacon in the darkness and the steady hand in moments of uncertainty. His knowledge of the underworld was unparalleled, making him the ideal shepherd for souls in their most vulnerable state.

Anubis was not just a passive escort. He actively engaged with the soul, offering wisdom and comfort. His presence was a constant reminder of the divine order and the righteousness of the path they walked. He was particularly present at critical junctures of the journey where the soul's fate hung in the balance. His guidance was crucial, for without it, the soul could easily lose its way, falling prey to the perils of the underworld. Anubis's main role was to ensure that each soul had a fair chance to reach its final destination, the Hall of Ma'at, where the ultimate judgment awaited it.

The climax of this journey was the Weighing of the Heart ceremony. In the presence of Osiris and a panel of judges, the soul's heart was placed on a scale opposite the feather of Ma'at, which symbolized truth and justice. Anubis, the impartial arbiter, oversaw this ceremony with a stern but fair gaze. He ensured that the scales were balanced. The heart represented the deeds the soul had committed throughout its life. A heart lighter or equal in weight to the feather signified a life lived with integrity and truth, granting the soul passage to the Field of Reeds, a place of eternal peace and pleasure.

A heart heavier than the feather would be burdened by wrongdoing and sin. This soul faced a dire fate. It was devoured by Ammit, the devourer of souls, condemning the soul to oblivion. The Weighing of the Heart ceremony was the ultimate test of a soul's purity and righteousness.

In the post-Late Period of ancient Egypt, spanning from 664 to 30 BCE, Anubis again underwent another transformation, adding a new dimension to his already complex character. During this era, Anubis was still revered as the god of funerary rites and the guardian of the dead, but he also became closely associated with necromancy. This aspect of Anubis highlights the Egyptians' deepening exploration into the mysteries of life, death, and the hereafter.

Anubis weighing the heart of the dead.[28]

Necromancy, the practice of communicating with the dead to predict the future or uncover hidden knowledge, became a part of certain religious and magical practices in Egypt. Anubis, with his intimate connection to the underworld and the afterlife, was naturally invoked in these rituals. He was seen as a powerful intermediary, a bridge between the living and the spirits of the deceased, as well as other deities who dwelled in the nether realm.

Demotic spells, written in the common script of the time, were often used to call upon Anubis in these necromantic practices. These spells were intricate and required a deep understanding of the rituals and language that were believed to hold sway in the supernatural world. Practitioners would perform elaborate ceremonies that often involved offerings, recitations, and specific gestures to invoke Anubis.

Upon his invocation, Anubis was believed to traverse the boundaries between the worlds. As a guide and protector in the underworld, he had unique access to spirits and gods who resided there. Those practicing necromancy would ask Anubis to fetch these spirits or gods since they sought their counsel or assistance. This could involve asking questions about the future, seeking guidance for important decisions, or even trying to gain knowledge about secret matters.

Anubis's portrayal as a jackal-headed god was itself steeped in symbolism. The jackal, an animal often seen around cemeteries, was associated with death and decay yet also with protection and guidance. Anubis's visage embodied these dual aspects, reflecting his role in guarding the dead and guiding them through the afterlife. Anubis was often shown holding the ankh, the symbol of life, and the scepter, which represented power and authority. These symbols highlighted his role as a giver of life in the afterlife and a deity capable of navigating the underworld.

Anubis vs Set

Osiris's death was felt by many, including the sun god Ra. In fact, Ra was the one who specifically requested that Anubis assist Isis in resurrecting Osiris. Since Anubis was extremely loyal to Isis, he did not hesitate to help. The resurrection process was said to have begun with the mummification of Osiris, which Anubis oversaw to ensure every phase was perfectly done. This was the very first time the Egyptians were introduced to mummification. Apart from preserving the body itself, the process also involved other important rituals. Among these was the Opening of the Mouth ceremony, a rite designed to ensure that Osiris could see, hear, breathe, and eat in the afterlife, effectively restoring his senses.

Of course, Anubis and the other gods were not free from obstacles. During the process, they had to face the schemes of Set, who was always watching their movements. When the god of chaos learned of the efforts to resurrect Osiris, he made haste to foil them. His chance came when Anubis had his hands full one day while working on embalming Osiris. At night, the god of embalming would leave the webet, the place where the embalming work took place, leaving Osiris's body alone with the guards. Seizing the opportunity, Set transformed himself into Anubis. He managed to convince the guards, allowing him to enter the webet and steal Osiris's body.

This theft was discovered by Anubis himself. Without wasting any time, he chased after the deceitful god of chaos. He knew he had to retrieve the body of Osiris. Set, realizing that Anubis was pursuing him, morphed into a bull. He confronted Anubis in this form, but the jackal-headed god proved to be stronger. Some sources say that Anubis succeeded in capturing and imprisoning Set, though this imprisonment was only for a short while.

This was not the last time the two gods would confront each other. Set transformed into a panther in order to steal the remains of Osiris again. However, Anubis had learned his lesson; ever since the first encounter, he had his eyes wide open for trouble. He knew Set would stop at nothing just so he could secure the throne for himself. Upon uncovering Set's plan, Anubis succeeded in capturing Set in his panther form. This time around, he branded him hundreds of times with a hot iron. This mythological tale is often cited as the reason why leopards have spots.

On the other hand, another account from a Ptolemaic papyrus known as Jumilhac tells us a different end. According to this version, Anubis was said to have skinned Set while he was in his leopard form. The jackal-headed god then wore his pelt as a trophy. Egyptologists and scholars view this as a symbol of Anubis's dominion over chaos and evil. This imagery was so powerful that it influenced Egyptian religious practices. Following the spread of this myth, priests began wearing leopard pelts as a symbol of their connection to Anubis and their role in maintaining order over chaos.

In modern times, Anubis is often portrayed as a malevolent deity, a figure shrouded in the darkness of death and mystery. This depiction, however, stands in stark contrast to the reverence and respect he commanded in ancient Egyptian culture. To the Egyptians, Anubis was not a symbol of fear or evil; instead, he was a revered guardian and guide, an essential figure in their spiritual and religious life.

Chapter 6: The Guardians of Order: Thoth and Ma'at

There was once a man who lived in Memphis. He did not know it yet, but he was just hours away from experiencing a life-changing event. Unlike many other Egyptians of his time, the man had never experienced poverty. He was born into a well-off family and seldom went through hardship. Yet, he had a strange addiction. The man had a habit of taking things that did not belong to him. Of course, he was not a thief by career. The man simply loved the thrill of stealing.

One day, the man stole a piece of jewelry from an unsuspecting merchant. He had been eyeing it for days, and finally, fueled by both greed and the lust for a fortune not his own, he snatched it and calmly walked away. Later on, as the man passed through the winding streets lined with sandstone houses and lively market stalls, his path inadvertently led him past a temple. Here, an image of a certain goddess caught his attention. It was a relief of Ma'at, the goddess whose very essence was the embodiment of truth and justice. Familiar to all Egyptians, her presence reminded them of the moral and cosmic order. However, the sight of Ma'at did not stir remorse in the man's heart. He continued walking home without feeling even the slightest hint of regret in his heart.

The goddess Ma'at adorning the feather of truth.[38]

As night fell, he was sitting alone, admiring the stolen jewelry. It was so intricately made that the moment its facets caught the light, the room was immediately filled with a dance of shadows and radiance. The man smiled. He saw the jewel as something more than just a trinket. He viewed it as a symbol of his skill and audacity. Satisfied with his work for the day, the man placed the jewelry aside and fell asleep.

Suddenly, the familiar comfort of his bed gave way to an ethereal realm. He noticed that he was no longer in his safe home but in the mysterious and foreboding world of the Du'at, the Egyptian underworld.

The transition from the world of the living to the Du'at was a journey shrouded in mystery and ancient lore. For a pharaoh, the passage to the afterlife was almost like a ceremonial voyage. He would be assisted by spells, sacred rituals, and opulent tombs designed to ease his journey to the realm beyond. However, for ordinary Egyptians, like our unnamed man, the journey was very different. It would be a sudden and disorienting shift completely devoid of grandeur or guidance.

The man ventured deeper into this unknown world, eventually encountering the many guardians of the underworld. He could feel himself shivering before these divine entities. All of them had a rather formidable appearance. They were part animal, part god. These entities were the ones who upheld the realm's sacred laws. They stood before imposing gates, their eyes piercing through him as if peeling back the layers of his soul. With each step, he felt the weight of his stolen treasures like chains around his heart.

The realms he traversed were as terrifying as they were wondrous. He walked across a vast desert where he witnessed dozens of lost souls wandering around. Each of them was lamenting the many regrets of their lives. One spoke of his own greed, while another expressed her regret for abandoning the gods. The man also came across a dark river whose waters were deep and still. Although the man could not see any dangerous creatures lurking underneath the water, he could feel a sense of unease slowly crawling at the back of his neck.

His steps eventually brought him to the assembly of gods. Each of them was a representation of the virtues upheld by Ma'at. Among them were Osiris, the lord of the underworld; Anubis, the guardian of the scales; Thoth, the scribe of the gods; and others who embodied the divine aspects of justice, truth, and order. Before these deities, the man was compelled to recite the Negative Confession, a declaration of innocence against the forty-two sins of Ma'at's code. With each confession, he finally felt the weight of his past actions.

Ammit, the devourer of souls.[34]

Only upon completing this confession did the true test begin: the Weighing of the Heart. The man watched in silent horror as, one by one, the souls were judged. Some were granted passage to the Field of Reeds, a peaceful paradise. Others, whose hearts were filled with wrongdoing, faced the grim fate of being devoured by Ammit, the devourer of souls.

A depiction of Aaru or the Field of Reeds.[35]

When his turn came, the man could feel his heart racing. The scales were then set, and finally, his heart was placed on one side. The feather of Ma'at was placed on the other. Suddenly, the balance tipped. His heart was heavy with the weight of his misdeeds. The sight of this caused the man to lose his ability to breathe. His panic worsened the moment he saw Ammit's fearsome jaws get closer to his face. Then, everything went dark. He jolted awake.

He had never experienced such a nightmare before. Panting and drenched in his own sweat, the man lay still on his bed. He then recalled the time he saw an image of Ma'at carved at the temple he passed by the day before and realized the gods were indeed watching him. The terror of the dream left a lasting mark on him. He made a solemn vow to amend his ways. He resolved to align his life with the principles of truth and justice, ensuring that the nightmarish vision the gods had given him would never manifest into reality.

The Concept of Ma'at in Ancient Egyptian Belief and as a Goddess

In the ancient Egyptian religion, Ma'at stood as the pillar of cosmic and societal order. She was more than just a goddess; she was also the embodiment of truth, balance, order, and justice. To the Egyptians, her influence could be felt in every aspect of existence, from the movement of the stars to the daily lives of mortals, be it the powerful pharaohs or common people. The concept of Ma'at was integral to maintaining harmony in the universe, as this harmony ensured the cyclical nature of life, from the flooding of the Nile to the transition of souls in the afterlife, continued to happen without disruption.

Ma'at was often depicted in human form as a woman with an ostrich feather (the feather of truth) atop her head. This feather represented the lightness and purity that truth brought to the soul. Temples dedicated to Ma'at were rare since her presence was more a part of the fabric of everyday life and state affairs rather than the focus of individual worship. Pharaohs, in particular, were seen as the earthly embodiments of Ma'at, and they were tasked with upholding her principles while ruling the kingdom.

Ma'at, as a goddess, was unique. She did not have the dramatic myths or narratives typical of other Egyptian deities. Instead, her power and influence were more abstract. As a symbol of moral and ethical righteousness, Ma'at was the touchstone against which all actions, both of deities and mortals, were measured. From the grandest temples to the humblest homes, her principles were the guiding force behind law, governance, and personal conduct. In religious ceremonies, offerings to Ma'at were common, as they symbolized the pharaoh's or an individual's commitment to upholding truth and balance in their reign and/or life.

The principles of Ma'at were not just religious doctrines but also a way of life. In societal terms, Ma'at represented the ideal state of affairs, where harmony prevailed and chaos was kept at bay. For the individual, living in accordance with Ma'at meant living a life of honesty, integrity, and moral righteousness. The concept of "living in Ma'at" was essential for one's personal well-being and prosperity.

Thoth

While Ma'at stood as a guardian of the underworld and a beacon of truth and justice, she was not alone in her vigilant watch over the realms of the afterlife. Alongside her, another deity played a role of equal magnitude and mystery. This was Thoth. To the ancient Egyptian people, he was the god of wisdom, writing, and, sometimes, the moon.

Thoth's depiction in ancient Egyptian art is striking. This deity had the body of a man and the head of an ibis, his sharp beak a symbol of the precision of thought and language. In his hand, he often held a scribe's palette and stylus, ready to record the deeds of mortals and gods alike.

Thoth's name and origin are deeply rooted in the ancient Egyptian belief system. His name, *Dhwty* in the Egyptian language, means "he who is like the ibis." The ibis was an elegant bird and was commonly seen along the Nile. It was revered for its wisdom, a trait Thoth himself personified.

Legends about Thoth's birth vary. Some claim that he was self-created at the beginning of time, while others suggest he emerged from the lips of Ra, the sun god. This birth narrative positions Thoth not only as a divine being but also as an intrinsic part of the cosmic order, as his very existence is tied to the creation of the universe.

The worship of Thoth dates back to the predynastic period. He grew in prominence as the Egyptian civilization evolved. His main worship center was in Hermopolis, a city that became synonymous with Thoth's cult. The reverence for Thoth in Hermopolis was not just limited to grand temples and elaborate rituals. It also manifested in a more tangible, albeit peculiar, form. Pilgrims who came to the city, particularly during festivals, would often buy mummified ibises and baboons. These were votive offerings and were given in the hope of earning Thoth's favor.

Thoth, the Egyptian god of wisdom.[36]

Thoth's appeal transcended social hierarchies. While he was especially popular among the royals, who saw him as a divine arbitrator and the keeper of cosmic balance, commoners also showed their devotion to him. In an era when literacy was limited to a select few, Thoth represented the pinnacle of knowledge and wisdom. To venerate Thoth was to aspire to these esteemed qualities. His popularity reached its zenith during the New Kingdom. In this era, Thoth was not just a god to be feared or appeased; he was also seen as a symbol of enlightenment, guiding the Egyptians in both their worldly pursuits and their spiritual endeavors.

Thoth played a crucial role in the shadowy realm of the Du'at, the ancient Egyptian underworld. In the solemn chamber where the hearts of the deceased were weighed against the feather of Ma'at, Thoth stood among the other gods as the impartial scribe. It was his divine duty to record the proceedings, keeping meticulous accounts of each soul's life and actions. As the scales tipped to reveal the truth, Thoth chronicled the outcome.

Thoth's role in the Book of the Dead is particularly illustrative of his importance. He is often depicted before the scales, quill and palette in hand, ready to inscribe the verdict. This critical function elevated Thoth to the status of a deity embodying truth and integrity. The Egyptians revered him for this impartiality, often expressing a desire to live a life "straight and true like Thoth."

Beyond his duties in the Hall of Truth, Thoth's influence in the underworld extended to his abode, known as the Mansion of Thoth. This was a sanctuary for souls. The Mansion of Thoth was seen as a safe haven, a place where souls could find respite and protection. It was here that Thoth, with his boundless knowledge, bestowed magic spells upon the souls, empowering them to face and overcome the demons that lurked in the underworld seeking to impede their journey to paradise. These spells were powerful incantations imbued with the wisdom and authority of Thoth. They served as a shield against the terrors of the Du'at.

The lore of Thoth as the creator of knowledge casts him in an even more magnificent light. Thoth was credited with the creation and mastery of several branches of knowledge that shaped the spiritual and intellectual landscape of ancient Egypt.

Thoth was revered as the originator of law, laying down the foundation for order and justice in society. He was seen as the ultimate arbitrator whose wisdom was indispensable in resolving conflicts and maintaining balance. His influence extended to magic, where he was regarded as the supreme magician whose knowledge of spells and incantations was unmatched. This aspect of Thoth resonated deeply with the Egyptian belief in the power of words and rituals to influence the natural and supernatural worlds.

Thoth's contributions were no less significant in philosophy. He was thought to be the one who crafted the fabric of Egyptian religious and philosophical thought, providing insights into the mysteries of existence and the cosmos. Science, too, fell under Thoth's domain. He was the measurer of the earth and the counter of the stars, a deity whose wisdom understood the inner workings of the universe.

However, perhaps the most enduring of Thoth's creations was writing. The god was attributed with the invention of hieroglyphics, the sacred script that not only recorded the history and culture of ancient Egypt but was also believed to hold magical powers. The ancient Egyptians believed that writing was more than a means of communication. They saw it as a divine gift from Thoth himself, enabling the preservation and dissemination of knowledge across generations.

Thoth's reputation as a god of wisdom and knowledge was not confined to the borders of Egypt. His influence reached the shores of Greece, where he was revered as Hermes Trismegistus. This syncretic figure, a blend of the Egyptian Thoth and the Greek Hermes, shows the existence of cross-cultural exchange between these two great civilizations. Hermes Trismegistus embodied the qualities of both gods, and he was revered as a messenger and a mediator.

In Greece, Thoth-Hermes Trismegistus was celebrated as the god of wisdom and the patron of esoteric knowledge. He influenced religious thought, alchemy, and the early foundations of science. The Greeks saw in Hermes Trismegistus a deity who transcended the physical world, offering a bridge to the divine and unlocking the secrets of the universe.

Thoth's role as the god of wisdom and the creator of knowledge was thus a cornerstone in the intellectual and spiritual heritage of Egypt and the wider ancient world. His teachings, whether in the form of religious texts, philosophical treatises, or scientific observations, were considered to be divine revelations, offering guidance and enlightenment to those who sought to understand the deeper truths of existence. In every stroke of a scribe's pen, in every incantation uttered by a magician, and in every decision made by a judge, the presence of Thoth was felt.

Thoth's wisdom and cunning not only earned him a revered place among the mortals but also made him a pivotal figure in the tales of gods. His involvement in the divine dramas of the Egyptian pantheon showcased his ingenuity and resourcefulness, making him an indispensable ally to the other gods. One such tale involves Ra and a particular deity—some claim her to be the sun god's daughter—known as the Distant Goddess.

In this legend, the Distant Goddess was said to be Hathor, also known as the Eye of Ra. She was the goddess of many things, including love, beauty, music, dancing, fertility, and pleasure. The story began when the goddess, in a fit of anger, momentarily broke away from the established order. Perhaps disenchanted and seeking solitude, she transformed into a fierce feline, a move that represented freedom and untamed nature. She fled into the desert, leaving behind her responsibilities and her father, Ra, the sun god. In her absence, a sense of imbalance pervaded, as if the earth itself yearned for her return.

Ra was deeply concerned by her absence and its effects on the land, so he turned to Thoth for assistance. Thoth, who was known for his wisdom and persuasive abilities, was tasked with the crucial mission of bringing her back.

The journey to retrieve the Distant Goddess was not one of brute force or coercion. Instead, Thoth used his skills of diplomacy and understanding. While disguised as either a baboon or a monkey, Thoth approached her. He recognized her grievances and acknowledged her autonomy. Through clever dialogue and patient negotiation, he persuaded her to return. One source claims the god had to persuade her 1,077 times before she agreed.

The return of the Distant Goddess brought rejuvenation to the world. Her return heralded the inundation of the Nile, an event that brought life-giving waters to the people of Egypt. However, the goddess's return was contingent on more than just the desire of Ra or the needs of the people. She had to be appeased and honored with jubilant festivities. Music, dancing, feasting, and drunken revelry were essential rituals to placate the goddess and ensure her benevolence.

Chapter 7: Horus the Falcon King

Isis was alone now that Osiris had departed to the land of the dead to preside over the souls of the deceased. Knowing that Set would do everything in his power to remain on the throne of Egypt, the goddess made haste to retreat into the shadows of the Nile Delta. She knew she had to protect her son, Horus, especially since Osiris himself had prophesied that their son would bring honor back to the family name. After enduring hours of extreme labor, Isis gave birth to Horus. She began raising him the best she could, putting his safety above all.

To avoid danger, the goddess chose to only emerge out of the secluded marshland at night. This was when she would go and search for food to keep herself and her only son alive. However, Isis was not alone. She was protected by a bodyguard of seven scorpions, which belonged to the goddess of healing and poison, Serket (who we will discuss further later on). However, Isis still had to be on alert at all times since Set had installed eyes nearly everywhere. While Isis was out looking for food, Horus would be left with Serket, who nurtured him. Horus eventually grew into a god of formidable stature.

Horus showed signs of divinity and extraordinary power the very moment he arrived in the world. One of his eyes was said to have glowed as bright as the sun, while the other appeared as luminous as the moon. He also had the head of a falcon, which represented the keen vision and soaring spirit of the bird. His physical prowess was impressive and was matched by his sharp intellect. The ancient Egyptians believed that his gaze could pierce through untruths. Later on, the people would depict the god wearing the double crown of Egypt, signifying his dominion over both the physical world and the celestial realm.

The son of Osiris and Isis also displayed a keen sense of awareness and unyielding spirit from an early age. As he grew up, Isis began instilling in him the virtues of justice, honor, and compassion. The goddess also taught him the secrets of the gods and filled his childhood with stories of the land. She worked hard to prepare him for the day when he claimed his throne. Of course, her teachings were not of vengeance or hatred; Isis taught him to understand the delicate balance that governs all existence.

Eventually, Horus developed traits that endeared him to all of creation. He was brave, not in the sense of a warrior but as one who faces the unknown with unwavering resolve. His wisdom was evident in his thoughtful demeanor. He always considered the consequences of his actions on the cosmic balance. And above all, he was just, a quality he held most dear since it reflected his inherent role as a future upholder of Ma'at, the ancient Egyptian concept of truth and order.

Meanwhile, the land of Egypt was plunged into turmoil under the rule of Set. The once flourishing kingdom, which had been nourished by the wise rule of Osiris and the nurturing care of Isis, withered under the grip of chaos and disorder.

Under Osiris, Egypt had been a land of plenty. The god-king, together with Isis, had introduced the art of agriculture and culture to humanity. Their reign was a golden era, marked by bountiful harvests and rivers teeming with fish. The fields of Egypt were lush with grain, and the granaries overflowed with the rewards of a well-tended earth. The people thrived. Their needs were fulfilled, and their lives were enriched by the blessings of their divine rulers.

But with Set upon the throne, the prosperous land transformed for the worse. Where there was once abundance, there was famine in the cities and villages. The Nile, which had faithfully nourished the land, flooded unpredictably or withheld its life-giving waters, leaving the fields parched and

Horus, the falcon-headed god.[27]

barren. Crops withered, and hunger crept into homes that had once known only plenty.

The skies mirrored the chaos below. Once clear and bright, they were often shrouded in ominous clouds, casting shadows over the land. Plagues sickened both livestock and people, adding to the growing despair.

Social order, which had been the centerpiece of Egyptian life under Osiris and Isis, greatly declined under Set's rule. Where there had been justice and fairness, now there was only the whim of a tyrant. Previously, the people looked toward the throne for guidance and protection, but with Set on top, they could only feel the heavy yoke of oppression. It became increasingly clear that the throne belonged to someone of pure heart—someone who could mirror the previous king. Perhaps a direct descendant of the great Osiris himself.

When Horus finally reached adulthood, he knew it was time to gather his strength, reclaim his birthright, and restore Egypt to its former glory. Horus was said to have first approached the gods to stake his claim. Standing before a court of the Great Ennead, which included Set himself and was presided by Ra, he laid forth his case. He pointed his finger at Set, claiming that he had unlawfully usurped the throne. He exclaimed that Egypt had been in turmoil under the god of chaos for too long and that it was time for Set to step down.

The gods listened intently as Horus made his plea. They saw in him the potential for a great king, one who could blend Osiris's just rule with his own unique strengths. Many viewed Horus as the beacon of hope that Egypt desperately needed.

Ra was not as easily swayed by his speech. While some suggested he had an issue with Horus's young age and inexperience, others whispered that the sun god actually harbored sympathy for Set. The god of chaos might have unleashed havoc across the kingdom, but he was a loyal companion in Ra's nightly battles against Apophis. The divine assembly failed to reach a consensus. Opinions were clearly divided.

Knowing that Horus would not leave empty-handed, Ra came up with a pronouncement. The decision of who would ascend to the throne of Egypt would not be made by divine decree alone. Instead, it would be determined through a series of contests between Horus and Set. The winner of these trials would prove their worthiness to rule and would be crowned as the rightful king.

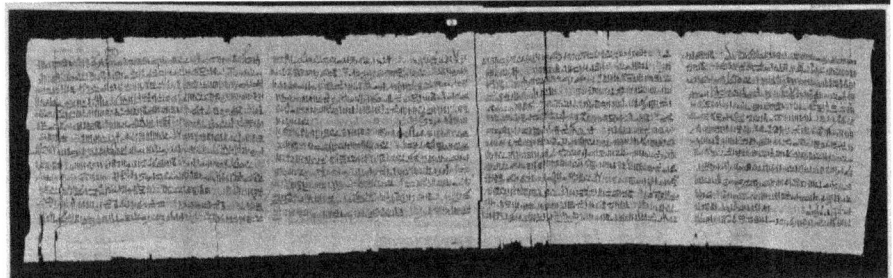
The manuscript detailing the events of "The Contendings of Horus and Set."[28]

The first trial was rather peculiar. It was chosen by none other than the god of chaos himself. The test was to see who among the two contending gods could remain underwater the longest. Both Set and Horus had to transform themselves into hippopotami before submerging themselves into the Nile. Whoever succeeded in remaining underwater for three consecutive months would be declared the winner.

When the day of the trial arrived, the banks of the Nile were alive with anticipation. Not only had the mighty gods and goddesses gathered to watch the trial, but the banks were also filled with spirits and creatures of all kinds. Set, ever confident, morphed first. His hippo form was massive, complete with thick skin and powerful jaws. When he snapped his jaws shut, a loud sound pierced the air, frightening even the mightiest of animals present. Then, Horus transformed, taking on the hefty and robust form of a hippopotamus. He did not display any act of boastful bravery like his uncle. Instead, he remained calm as he surveyed his surroundings.

After being given the green light to begin the trial, Horus and Set plunged into the Nile. Silence replaced the anticipation in the air as the two gods disappeared beneath the surface. The first few days passed slowly, yet neither god was planning on coming to the surface anytime soon. They both maintained their positions underwater, putting their endurance to the ultimate test. When days turned into weeks, the interest and anxiety among the gods grew.

Isis watched the test with growing concern. She was beginning to feel torn between her maternal instincts and the rules of the contest. Eventually, the goddess chose to intervene. Using her magic, she crafted a copper harpoon. She then stealthily approached the Nile and hurled the harpoon into the depths, hoping to hit Set and disturb his focus.

Unfortunately, her aim was miscalculated. Instead of piercing Set, the harpoon struck her own son. However, Isis was quick enough to correct her mistake. Again, she prepared another harpoon and hurled it directly at Set. This time around, the harpoon found its mark, wounding Set. Perhaps startled and in pain, the god of chaos rose to the surface, surprising many.

In a turn of events, Set went to Isis. He did not approach the goddess in a rage. Instead, he played on their familial ties and asked her to heal his wounds. Although she was loyal to Horus, Isis eventually relented after finding herself swayed by her brother's pleas. The goddess healed Set's injuries. Of course, this did not go unnoticed. Horus emerged from the Nile, ready to express his fury following his mother's actions. Feeling betrayed, Horus impulsively decapitated Isis, shocking the entire crowd of gods on the banks of the river.

Thankfully, Thoth was present during the episode. Ever the mediator and preserver of order, he intervened. Thoth made use of his precious knowledge of magic and healing to save Isis. According to some accounts, Thoth replaced Isis's severed head with that of a cow, which symbolized her nurturing and maternal attributes, thus preserving her life and divinity.

As for Horus, he retreated to a mountain. The angry god was hoping he could find solace after going through the test and being betrayed by his mother. Little did he know, but Set had been following his every movement. Taking opportunity of Horus's vulnerable state—he was beyond exhausted at that time—Set gouged out Horus's left eye.

Interestingly, this act not only intensified their rivalry; it also symbolized yet another natural occurrence. The left eye of Horus came to represent the waxing and waning phases of the moon. When his eye was taken away and damaged, it was associated with the new moon when the moon was not visible. The waxing moon, as it gained visibility, represented the eye being gradually restored, and the full moon signified the complete restoration of his eyes.

Horus, now injured and weakened, was tended to by Hathor. The goddess of love and beauty, known for her healing abilities, took Horus under her care. She nursed him back to health, tending to his wounds and aiding in the restoration of his lost eye.

The rivalry between the two contenders did not stop there. After recovering, Horus made sure to make a move; he was not planning on letting Set get away forever. This next episode came to be known as the infamous lettuce scene. According to tradition, Set had come up with a certain scheme. He hoped to discredit Horus by asserting his dominance sexually. The story goes that Set snuck into Horus's tent to sexually abuse him. Horus, however, had already devised a strategy to thwart his uncle's devious plan. He quietly caught Set's seed in his hand. Horus did not confront Set immediately but instead sought the counsel of his mother, Isis.

The goddess devised a plan to turn the situation to Horus's advantage. She advised Horus to dispose of Set's seed in a way that would prevent it from being used against him. Following her guidance, Horus cast the seed into the river, ensuring that it would not serve as evidence of Set's dominance.

Of course, the plan did not end there. Isis then helped Horus craft his own seed and secretly placed it on Set's favorite food, which was lettuce. The plan worked without a hitch, and Set consumed the lettuce containing Horus's seed. When the time came for the gods to convene and judge the rightful ruler of Egypt, Set confidently proclaimed to the court that he had performed an act of dominance over Horus. Their stunned silence was broken when Horus stepped forward to deny the claim. He told the other gods that he was the one who had performed the act of dominance over Set. The gods did not know whose words were true, so they turned to Thoth to uncover the truth.

Thoth, using his divine abilities, called forth the seed of Set, expecting it to respond from within Horus. However, much to Set's surprise and embarrassment, it answered from the river, revealing his failure to dominate Horus. Thoth then called upon the seed of Horus. To the shock of many, the seed responded from within Set. This revelation turned the tables. Set, who had sought to humiliate Horus, found himself disgraced. The assembled gods laughed at Set's misfortune, and his claim to the throne was greatly weakened.

Still, their rivalry persisted for at least eighty years. The entire time, Ra continued to withhold his support from Horus, denying the son of Osiris his rightful claim to the throne. As a result, Egypt continued to spiral, as it suffered from mismanagement and neglect caused by Set. Isis could not bear to see the rivalry continue between the two. The stalemate had to end one way or the other, and Horus must sit on the throne. So, she transformed herself into a beautiful woman and made her way to Set's palace. Here, she began weeping, hoping to catch Set's attention.

Just as she suspected, the god of chaos was immediately drawn to the sight of this beautiful woman. Set asked her about the cause of her tears, to which Isis quickly spun a tale of woe. She told him of a cruel yet powerful man who had wronged her and her young son. She spoke of a story where the man denied them their rightful inheritance. Her story, though a fabrication, was laced with poignant details and delivered with such conviction that it stirred Set's emotions.

Set declared that such injustice was intolerable. He proclaimed that the man responsible for the young woman's suffering deserved severe punishment. He was so angry that he even swore a solemn oath to seek out this unjust man and cast him out of the lands. This was the moment Isis had been waiting for. She revealed her true identity, and unbeknownst to Set, they were not alone. Isis had gathered the other gods to witness Set's proclamations. Just like that, Set had unwittingly condemned himself. His promise to punish the man who caused the young woman's sorrow was, in fact, a self-indictment, as he was the one who had usurped the throne and caused suffering to Horus and Isis.

The irony of the situation was not lost on the assembled deities. Set, known for his cunning and trickery, had been outwitted by Isis's scheme. Ra, who had for so long resisted acknowledging Horus as the rightful king, could no longer deny the justice of his claim. The other gods, who had been divided in their support, now rallied behind Horus. Isis's intervention had not only exposed Set's hypocrisy but had also highlighted the righteousness of Horus's cause.

With Horus now on the throne, Egypt experienced an era of prosperity. Gone were the days of constant hunger, turmoil, and suffering. Horus's ascension to the throne was a moment of triumph, not just for him but for the ideals he represented: justice, rightful rule, and the restoration of order.

As for Set, he had to face the consequences of his actions. He was eventually banished to the dry and barren desert beyond the borders of Egypt. There is another tale that narrates his fate. According to this version of the myth, Set was presented before Horus in chains. To the surprise of many, Horus did not choose revenge. He understood the importance of cosmic balance and released Set instead of punishing him. Horus acknowledged that chaos, as represented by Set, was an essential part of the natural order. He held to the belief that the world needed both stability and upheaval to maintain harmony. Set willingly retreated to the desert instead of being banished.

Horus's reign was one of spiritual and cultural rejuvenation. As a deity closely associated with the sky, the sun, and kingship, Horus became a symbol of power, vigor, and legitimacy. This connection between Horus and the monarchy was deeply ingrained in the Egyptian concept of divine kingship. The pharaohs of Egypt, regarded as living gods themselves, identified strongly with Horus. They were seen as earthly embodiments of the falcon-headed god, reigning with his authority, might, and divine right. This identification lent a sacred dimension to their rule, reinforcing their status as intermediaries between the gods and the people.

Upon their death, the pharaohs were then associated with Osiris, the god of the afterlife and resurrection. This transformation from being Horus in life to Osiris in death was integral to the Egyptian belief in the afterlife and the cyclical nature of kingship and divinity. This belief system reinforced the pharaoh's divine status and the perpetuity of his rule, even in the afterlife.

Temples dedicated to Horus rose majestically along the Nile. They served as places of worship and as centers of learning and administration. The cult of Horus played a significant role in the religious life of the Egyptians, influencing rituals, festivals, and the arts.

Chapter 8: Serpent Magic and Transformation: Wadjet and Sobek

Many centuries before Egypt rose as the unified and powerful civilization that we remember today, the kingdom was a divided nation split into two distinct regions: Upper and Lower Egypt. Each region had its own unique cultural and political identity. Even the crown worn by their rulers (the term pharaoh was first used for Egyptian kings in the New Kingdom) were not the same. Those who had power in Lower Egypt (northern Egypt) wore the red crown known as the Deshret, while rulers of Upper Egypt (southern Egypt) adorned the tall white crown known as the Hedjet. Of course, these crowns were not just regal ornaments. They were also worn as powerful symbols of the ruler's authority and their connection to the gods.

WOODEN STATUETTES OF SENUSERT I., FROM LISHT.

The Hedjet crown of Upper Egypt (left) and the Deshret crown of Lower Egypt (right).[20]

The unification of Upper and Lower Egypt happened sometime around 3150 BCE. This unity brought about major changes across the land. It brought political and territorial cohesion, as well as a blending of cultural and religious symbols. One of the most prominent of these symbols was the Pschent. Often known simply as the double crown, it combined both elements of the Deshret and Hedjet. The Pschent, with its distinctive red and white elements, symbolized the ruler's dominion over both regions.

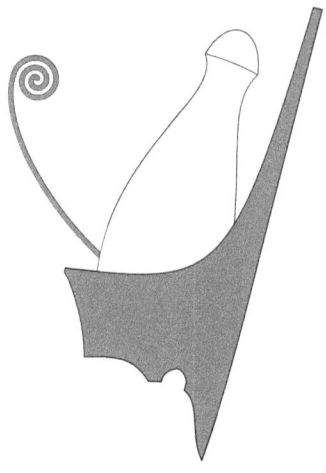

The double crown of unified Egypt.[80]

Central to the imagery of the pharaohs and their divine authority was the Uraeus, a stylized representation of a rearing cobra. Often affixed to the ruling pharaoh's headdress, the Uraeus symbolized royal authority, divine protection, and the fearsome power of the monarch. The rearing cobra was also a representation of the pharaoh's ability to ward off enemies who threatened his kingdom and evil spirits.

Tutankhamun's mask featuring a Uraeus.[81]

But why exactly did the Egyptians choose the cobra as the Uraeus? The significance of the Uraeus was, in fact, closely linked to a goddess known as Wadjet, which has been identified as one of the oldest deities in the Egyptian pantheon.

Wadjet, whose name meant "the green one," was a goddess whose influence and worship spanned the history of ancient Egyptian religion and culture. Initially a local goddess of the city Per-Wadjet (known to the Greeks as Buto), an important site in prehistoric Egypt, Wadjet's presence and significance evolved dramatically over the centuries. In her earliest representations during the predynastic period, Wadjet was depicted as a cobra, sometimes entwined around a papyrus stem, which perhaps symbolized her protective and nurturing nature.

A representation of Wadjet as a snake.[33]

As time progressed, depictions of Wadjet underwent a fascinating transformation. She was often portrayed as a woman with the head of a snake. Scholars suggest that this was a reflection of her dual nature as being both nurturing and fierce. At times, the Wadjet appeared as a lion-headed goddess, complete with the Uraeus on her head. This alternative image possibly signified royal power and authority. While her primary sacred animal was the cobra, the Late Period brought about an intriguing addition: the ichneumon. The ichneumon, a mongoose-like creature revered for its ability to kill snakes and crush crocodile eggs, became a sacred animal of Wadjet during this period.

The integration of the ichneumon into the worship of Wadjet was part of a broader pattern of religious syncretism prevalent during the Late Period. The deities of the Delta cities of Khem (Letopolis) and Per-Wadjet exemplified this trend. In these centers, the ichneumon, originally a sacred animal of Horus of Khem, was incorporated into the veneration of Wadjet of Per-Wadjet.

The reverence for the ichneumon in relation to Wadjet was distinct from that of other sacred animals. In artistic and religious representations, ichneumons were occasionally included in statuettes of Wadjet, particularly in her lion-headed form. These statuettes depicted the goddess seated on a throne, usually crowned by the Uraeus.

These statuettes often had a practical and spiritual function. The throne or the base attached to it, which was typically hollow, contained a mummified ichneumon. This practice reflected the ancient Egyptians' belief in the sacredness of animals and their role in the religious and spiritual realms.

The origins of the worship of Wadjet lay in Lower Egypt, where she was revered as the personification of the region. In fact, her temple in Per-Wadjet was not just a center of worship but also housed an oracle, believed by some to be a precursor to the oracle tradition in ancient Greece. This oracle was often consulted by pharaohs and commoners alike.

Depictions of Wadjet can be seen on the walls of various temples across Egypt. One notable example is in the Tomb of Nefertari, the wife of Ramesses II, where Wadjet is depicted as a winged cobra hovering protectively above Anubis. Her presence in such important burial sites underscored her role as a guardian deity. Additionally, Wadjet had a temple at the ancient site of Imet (now Tell Nebesha) in the Nile Delta, where she was worshiped as the Lady of Imet. Over time, she formed part of a triad with Min (another one of the oldest Egyptian gods associated with fertility and harvest) and Horus.

Wadjet depicted in the Tomb of Nefertari above Anubis.[83]

Wadjet's counterpart was Nekhbet, another ancient deity who was often depicted alongside her. Nekhbet was represented as a vulture and was primarily associated with Upper Egypt, in contrast to Wadjet's affiliation with Lower Egypt. Together, Wadjet and Nekhbet were known as the "Two Ladies," a title embodying the unification of Upper and Lower Egypt. This epithet, Nebty, was frequently used in a pharaoh's title, symbolizing the pharaoh's sovereignty over both regions.

Nekhbet as depicted in the tomb of Ramesses III.[84]

The roles of the Two Ladies extended beyond the symbolism of unified Egypt. According to some versions, Wadjet and Nekhbet were also seen as key figures during the time when Isis was protecting her son Horus. According to legend, Wadjet was responsible for transforming parts of the Nile Delta into lush, papyrus-filled wetlands. She caused the papyrus plant to grow thick and tall, acting as a natural barrier. This was done to protect Isis and Horus from the prying eyes of Set.

Of course, apart from acting as protection for the divine mother and son, the papyrus plant served as one of Egypt's most precious resources. It was also highly sought after by not just the Egyptians but also those who came from beyond the continent. The plant was used to make paper, which was important for recording history, culture, and governmental administrative duties. The papyrus swamps also played a critical ecological role, supporting a diverse range of wildlife and serving as a natural barrier against invaders.

Nekhbet and Wadjet played a hand in nurturing the young Horus, especially when Isis was not around. They nurtured the young god physically and spiritually. Together, Nekhbet and Wadjet imparted strength and wisdom to Horus, both of which he would later use against Set and during his reign on the throne of Egypt.

Sobek, the Crocodile God

It was common for the ancient Egyptians to see the divine in the most formidable of creatures. Take the Nile crocodiles. These fearsome beasts inhabited the river's murky depths and were held in high regard by the Egyptian civilization rather than despised for their vicious nature. To them, these crocodiles were considered sacred. It was of the utmost importance to please them if they wished not to taste their wrath. To appease these beasts, the Egyptians prayed to a certain deity, hoping they could calm the crocodiles and safeguard themselves from harm.

This particular deity was known as Sobek. Many view Sobek as the Egyptian god of protection. The truth, however, is rather more complex. While the crocodile god was considered a benevolent creature, he could also be unpredictable. While he was known to have the ability to ward off evil and protect the innocent, there were instances when Sobek displayed his aggressiveness and violence. Perhaps this was the very reason why he was also associated with military prowess.

Sobek had two different appearances. Most of the time, the god would appear as a muscular man with the head of a crocodile. To symbolize his divinity and power, Sobek wore an elaborate ceremonial headdress. Known as the Hemhem crown, it was said to have been a gift to the crocodile god by Ra. It was given as a reward for his military feats. Typically, the crown was often depicted with a ram's horns, a sun disk, and the Uraeus (the symbol of a rearing cobra, signifying divine authority). Sobek could also be depicted entirely as a crocodile. This version of the god was usually seen in temple reliefs that narrated stories of his role as the protector of the Nile.

At times, the crocodile god could be seen holding the ankh, which the Egyptians saw as a symbol of fertility. His Was scepter also denoted his royal god status, while the solar disk above his head linked him to the sun.

A relief from the Temple of Kom Ombo featuring Sobek in his crocodile-headed form.[85]

Although the god was known for his unpredictable nature, it is not fair to dismiss how important he was to the Nile. Certain ancient sources suggest that Sobek was the very god who created the Nile River. The river was believed to have originated from his own sweat. Because of his status as the god of fertility, the water lily could also appear in his depictions, symbolizing regeneration and rebirth.

Sobek's worship was especially prominent in areas where crocodiles called home. His worship was mainly focused in Shedet, later known as Crocodilopolis. This major cult center, situated in the lush Faiyum region, became the heart of the worship of Sobek, especially during the Middle Kingdom when his significance in the Egyptian pantheon notably increased.

The temples dedicated to Sobek in Crocodilopolis were unique, as they often housed live crocodiles that were raised for religious purposes. These crocodiles were considered to be living incarnations of Sobek himself. Because of that, they were treated with great reverence and care since they were thought to be sacred beings. The death of a crocodile was not taken lightly. More often than not, the ancient Egyptians performed rituals for these sacred crocodiles. These rituals were usually done at the main temple in Crocodilopolis, with the crocodiles being treated as the earthly manifestations of Sobek.

The remains of crocodiles were treated with absolute care as well. They were mummified and stored safely. Interestingly, some of these mummified crocodiles have been found with baby crocodiles in their mouths or on their backs. This aspect of the crocodile's behavior, diligent in caring for its young, was preserved through mummification, symbolizing the protective and nurturing nature of Sobek.

The mummified crocodiles were not only kept in temples. They were also sometimes buried with pharaohs or nobles. It was believed that these sacred animals would continue to provide protection in the afterlife, guarding the deceased against any harm.

Mummified crocodiles at the Temple of Kom Ombo.[56]

In addition to Crocodilopolis, another key location in the worship of Sobek was Kom Ombo. This site was initially shared by Sobek and Horus as patrons. However, a myth recounts that a disagreement between the two deities led to Sobek expelling Horus from the temple. This act brought misfortune to the area, manifesting as a plague. Realizing the gravity of his actions, Sobek called upon Horus to return, restoring their joint patronage over Kom Ombo. The temple became a dual sanctuary, honoring both Sobek and Horus.

Aside from Crocodilopolis, Sobek was also worshiped by people in Kom Ombo. Initially, the site was under the protection of two gods: Sobek and Horus. However, legend has it that the two deities once became embroiled in a heated disagreement. This resulted in Sobek expelling Horus from Kom Ombo. Unfortunately, Sobek's impulsive action brought misfortune to the area. A plague razed the population, killing even the strongest humans. After finally realizing that the plague was the consequence of his actions, Sobek recalled Horus, restoring their joint patronage over Kom Ombo. From then on, the temple at Kom Ombo continued as a dual sanctuary. Those who visited were allowed to pay their respects to both Horus and Sobek.

Similar to Osiris, Anubis, and other prominent gods of the Egyptian pantheon, Sobek went through a period of transformation over time. The ancient Egyptians began associating Sobek more with the sun god Ra. They eventually merged these two divine figures, creating Sobek-Ra. This elevated Sobek's status further. Besides being honored for creating and protecting the Nile, Sobek was also linked to the great power of the sun.

Sobek's influence could be felt in various aspects of Egyptian culture, particularly in royal ideology. One of the most striking examples is the story of Sobekneferu, the first recorded female pharaoh of the kingdom. Having ruled at the close of the Twelfth Dynasty, her name means the "Beauty of Sobek." The pharaoh's decision to include Sobek in her name showed the high esteem in which the crocodile deity was held during her time. Not only did this indicate her ultimate devotion to Sobek, but Sobekneferu was also seeking divine endorsement to reinforce her authority in both the political and religious realms. Although her reign was relatively brief, it marked a period in which the cult of Sobek (especially the version where he was merged with Ra) gained more prominence within state worship and royal identity.

While the inclusion of Sobek's name in her title can be interpreted as a reflection of her desire to align her rule with the attributes associated with Sobek—strength, protection, and rejuvenation—some sources also suspected that this action served a critical political purpose. Although Egyptian women had more rights compared to other ancient cultures like the Greeks or the Romans, to rule a kingdom as a female pharaoh was still a challenge. Female pharaohs often found themselves facing the challenging task of asserting their authority in a predominantly male-dominated sphere. Therefore, this strategic use of Sobek's name can be interpreted as Sobekneferu's way of infusing her rule with a sense of masculinity and divine power, characteristics traditionally associated with male pharaohs. It was a means to solidify her position and proclaim her power in a society where female pharaohs were rarities.

Of course, Sobekneferu was not the only female leader known to have assumed aspects of male divinity to assert her rule. The same could be said about Hatshepsut, who ruled much later. Hoping to assert her authority in a patriarchal society, Hatshepsut famously donned the regalia and symbols of a male ruler in official ceremonies. Even her statues were often depicted with a false beard and a nemes headdress, the striped headcloth typically worn by male kings of Egypt. However, despite Hatshepsut's many contributions to the kingdom, the pharaoh failed to escape the act of *damnatio memoriae*, the condemnation of memory. Her inscriptions and monuments were later destroyed by her rivals who wished to erase her from history; this clearly failed since her name is known to us today.

Despite the challenges faced by Sobekneferu and Hatshepsut in asserting their authority in a patriarchal society, it is important to note that Egypt had several other female rulers who successfully navigated the complexities of leadership in ancient times. These women demonstrated remarkable resilience and adaptability, often utilizing similar strategies to assert their rule and leave their mark on Egyptian history.

Sobek's evolution from a feared deity of the Nile to a figure embodying both protection and royal authority, especially in his merged form with Ra, underscores the Egyptians' deep connection to and reverence for the natural world and its deities. His influence, evident in the reigns of pharaohs like Sobekneferu, highlights the role of gods in legitimizing and guiding rulership.

Chapter 9: Lesser-Known Deities: A Case Study

While the likes of Osiris, Isis, and Ra often dominate the narrative with their prominent roles and well-known legends, there is a group of lesser-known but equally intriguing gods and goddesses who wielded a lot of influence in various aspects of ancient Egyptian culture. This particular chapter is reserved for these deities. We will talk about Seshat, the goddess of writing; Khnum, the divine potter; Serket, the scorpion goddess of healing and protection; and Babi, the fierce baboon god of the underworld.

A carving of Seshat at the Temple of Luxor, dating from 1250 BCE.[87]

Seshat, the Goddess of Many Responsibilities

Seshat played an important role in the daily and ceremonial life of this ancient civilization. Her name, translating to "female scribe," hints at her primary role in Egyptian society.

Seshat often appeared as a woman wearing a leopard skin draped over her robe. Her headdress was rather unique. She did not wear an elaborate crown full of precious stones and gems but rather a simple seven-pointed star arched by a crescent bow. Unfortunately, not much evidence survived that could explain the meaning behind her appearance. Some scholars suggest that her crown represented her connection to the heavens or perhaps was a symbol of precision and dexterity. Others claim it indicated her celestial stature. Her leopard skin was linked to power and control over danger. Leopards were seen as fierce predators.

Even her origins are shrouded in mystery. Some claimed she was related to the god of wisdom and writing, Thoth—she was either his wife or daughter. This connection is further emphasized by the differing views regarding the development of the writing system in ancient Egypt. While some sources attribute this monumental advancement to Thoth, others believe it was Seshat who created it. Only then did Thoth teach it to humanity. According to Egyptologist Richard H. Wilkinson, Seshat frequently appeared in reliefs and inscriptions, especially those dating from the Early Dynastic Period, as the goddess of measurements and writing, which clearly indicated her significance from very early on.

Seshat was also considered the patroness of libraries and librarians. She was said to have played a major role in the maintenance and preservation of knowledge. Her responsibilities included record-keeping, accounting, measurements, and census-taking. Of course, her role as a record-keeper was not limited to mundane affairs. During the Middle Kingdom era, she documented the spoils of war, including animals and captives, and kept track of tributes related to the king. During the New Kingdom, her association with the pharaoh became more pronounced, as she was believed to have recorded the years of his reign and the jubilee festivals, particularly the Sed festival, a ceremony that celebrated the continued rule and rejuvenation of the pharaoh.

Seshat was credited as the keeper of the House of Life, which was an institution that functioned as a library, university, and research center. This was where one could find an array of spiritual and practical knowledge in both written and pictorial forms. Of course, the goddess's influence was not only limited to writing and record-keeping. Seshat was also revered in the realm of architecture and construction; she was thought to be the patroness of builders. Legend has it that Seshat played a role in assisting pharaohs in the "stretching the cord" ritual, a foundational ceremony for temple-building that involved laying out the architectural plan.

In the realm of the dead, Seshat was seen as a friend of the deceased. At times, her image appeared alongside Nephthys in scenes of restoring the limbs of the departed.

Interestingly, despite her many responsibilities and the significance of her role, Seshat never had her own temples, cults, or formal worship. However, the high value placed on writing and construction in Egyptian society meant that she was venerated widely through everyday acts and daily rituals. From the Early Dynastic Period to the rule of the Ptolemaic dynasty, her presence was a constant in the lives of the ancient Egyptians. In this way, Seshat's influence, though less conspicuous than that of other deities, was deeply embedded in the culture and spirituality of ancient Egypt, leaving a lasting imprint on the civilization.

Khnum, the Ram-Headed God Who Shaped Mankind

Khnum was yet another one of the Egyptian gods depicted with the head of an animal; he had the head of a ram. Primarily recognized as the guardian of the source of the Nile, Khnum carried a responsibility that linked him to the life-giving properties of the river. In ancient Egypt, a ram was seen as a symbol of fertility and strength. Therefore, his depiction was fitting for a god believed to have control over the Nile's inundation. Khnum's guardianship over this process was critical to the survival and prosperity of ancient Egyptians, making him a deity of immense importance, particularly to those whose lives were closely tied to the river and its cycles.

A depiction of the ram-headed god, Khnum.[88]

Khnum's worship centers were primarily located at the First Cataract of the Nile, particularly on the island of Elephantine. Here, at the supposed source of the Nile, one could find a few of his temples and shrines. They were typically constructed and cared for by those whose lives were inextricably linked to the river. Without Khnum, their lives would not be prosperous, so it was important to hold the god in high regard.

Interestingly, Khnum was revered by the ancient Egyptians as the god of creation. According to tradition, he was believed to have been the divine potter who molded humans on his potter's wheel. After shaping a person from clay, Khnum breathed life into it, giving them a ka or a spirit. This scene of creation often made an appearance in temple reliefs and art. Typically, Khnum would be depicted by his potter's wheel as he carefully shaped an individual. Other ancient sources credited the ram-headed god with the creation of the "first egg of the world." This narrative placed him at the very heart of the universe's genesis, as this particular divine egg was believed to be the source of all creation, including life, the sun, and the cosmos.

A relief of Khnum creating a human being on his divine potter's wheel.[89]

The most enthralling story involving the ram-headed god is the one linked to Pharaoh Djoser and a great famine that struck the kingdom during his reign. This particular event was recorded clearly on the Famine Stela, which survived the test of time. According to this ancient source, Egypt once suffered a severe famine that plagued its people for seven years. Djoser, who was pharaoh at the time, spent day and night trying to save his people from the catastrophe. Seeing no other way, the pharaoh turned to divine intervention. He prayed to Khnum, hoping the god could assist in ending the drought.

Legend has it that the pharaoh had a dream afterward. In his sleep, he was met with the ram-headed deity, who promised the pharaoh to end the suffering should he agree to a condition. Khnum instructed Djoser to rebuild and fix the dilapidated temple of Khnum on Elephantine. After being awoken from his mysterious dream, Djoser did not waste any time doing exactly what the god had instructed him. He launched a reconstruction project to repair the temple, and just as Khnum had promised, Egypt was immediately healed. The annual flooding finally came to revitalize the crops, restoring the kingdom's agricultural abundance and saving the people from terrible hunger.

Djoser was not the only pharaoh whose story intertwined with Khnum. The female queen, Hatshepsut, was also said to have dealings with the ram-headed god. According to this story, Amun-Ra, disguised as Thutmose I (Hatshepsut's father), visited her mother. It was from this divine union that Hatshepsut was conceived. Khnum was thought to have been the one who breathed life into Hatshepsut, imbuing her with the essence of divinity and kingship. This narrative not only portrays Khnum's role as a giver of life, but it also ties him to the legitimization of royal power, something a female pharaoh needed since they had to navigate a patriarchal society to assert her authority.

Khnum's influence declined over time, overshadowed by other more prominent deities like Ra, Amun, and Osiris. However, the god's name was never completely erased in the story of ancient Egypt. His name was invoked by the Egyptians once in a while, and inscriptions of him survived for many centuries.

Serket, the Protective Scorpion Goddess

Serket, whose name means "she who causes the throat to breathe," was a multifaceted goddess who many agree transcends the simple categorization often found in ancient mythologies. Though there are no mythological tales detailing the goddess's origin unlike many deities in Egyptian mythology, her influence and presence in ancient Egyptian culture and religion are indeed vast. She had been worshiped largely in Lower Egypt since the Predynastic Period.

The scorpion goddess, Serket as seen in the Tomb of Nefertari.[40]

Although her origin and background remain a subject of debate among scholars, historians, and Egyptologists, Serket's depictions are rather rich and symbolic. More often than not, she appeared on the walls of temples and tombs as a female human with a scorpion sitting on her head. Other times, Serket was depicted as a scorpion with the head of a woman. Scholars suggest that this duality of human and scorpion form meant she was a goddess who mediated between the natural and supernatural worlds.

The most popular myth featuring Serket was the one involving Isis and her son, Horus. This particular myth offers a glimpse into her protective and vengeful sides. The story goes that Serket played a role in assisting Isis with protecting Horus from the wrath of the god of chaos, Set. It was believed that Isis herself was protected by seven of Serket's scorpions. Three scorpions named Petet, Tjetet, and Matet would scout ahead, ensuring Isis and Horus could pass safely. Two more, Masetet and Mesetetef, would remain by her side, while another two, Befen and Tefen (considered the fiercest of all seven scorpions), guarded the goddess from the rear in case Set ever planned an ambush from behind.

There was a time when Isis, in the disguise of a poor woman, journeyed to an unknown town. Here, she begged for some food and shelter for the night. However, Isis was not met with kindness. Instead, she had to face the scorn of a wealthy noblewoman who slammed the door on the disguised goddess, denying her hospitality. Serket was said to have witnessed the incident through the eyes of her scorpions. She was infuriated. Serket commanded her most loyal and fiercest scorpion, Tefen, to teach the noblewoman a lesson for her unkindness.

Tefen had the other scorpions surrender their poison to him, creating one that was strong enough to kill a human. He planned to inject the poison not into the noblewoman herself but her son.

As for Isis, she eventually found compassion from a poor peasant woman. Although she did not have much to offer, the woman gave the goddess a simple meal and offered her a bed to rest for the night. Delighted, Isis sat and ate with the woman that night. This was the moment Tefen had been waiting for. Knowing that Isis was safe for the moment, the scorpion was able to leave her side and exact revenge—or a lesson—on the noblewoman. Tefen stung the noblewoman's son, who, within seconds, dropped unconscious to the floor. Panicked, the noblewoman scrambled to help her son, attempting to revive him to no avail.

The noblewoman's despair eventually led her to Isis. The goddess, known for her compassion and motherly attributes, chose to heal the child despite the earlier rebuff. Legend has it that Isis invoked the secret names of the scorpions, neutralizing the poison with her powerful healing magic. This act of mercy not only revived the innocent child but also transformed the noblewoman's heart. Feeling ashamed of her earlier actions, she offered Isis her wealth as a token of gratitude.

Serket, who had been observing these events from the swampy marshland, felt remorse for her hasty decision to harm the innocent child. From then on, she vowed to protect all children.

Serket as a scorpion.⁴¹

Serket also played a crucial role in the underworld. The scorpion goddess was tasked with overseeing the souls of the deceased. The Egyptians believed that Serket's magical abilities could help the dead breathe again as they were reborn from their bodies, hence the meaning behind her name. She was both a rewarder of the justified and a punisher of the unworthy. While some believed that the unworthy were condemned straight to oblivion when their heart was devoured by Ammit, others believed that instead of ceasing to exist, their souls would be forever tormented by Serket.

However, Serket's wrath was not confined only to the netherworld. On earth, she and her scorpions would often wander the vast lands, exacting retribution on those who preyed on the innocent or engaged in wickedness. Interestingly, the venom of her scorpions varied in intensity. Some scorpion stings could only cause pain, while others had the capability to cause breathlessness or, worse, bring about their death.

As a goddess associated with death, she played a role in safeguarding the internal organs of the dead, particularly the intestines, which were associated with poison. She protected Qebehsenuef, one of the four sons of Horus, who was in charge of the intestines in the canopic jars.

Despite being categorized as a lesser goddess, Serket held a revered position in Egyptian religion. True, she did not have grand temples built in her honor. Yet, Serket had loyal followers. Known as the Followers of Serket, they were typically made up of physicians and healers adept in both medical and spiritual practices. Her cult was open to both men and women. They were typically known for their proficiency in medicine and the rites of Serket, which involved invoking her for healing. Spells in her name were commonly used for driving out poisons and ensuring good health.

Babi, the Bloodthirsty Baboon God

The ancient Egyptians considered the hamadryas baboon a sacred animal. Distinguishable by its grey streak of hair, this species of baboon was thought to have possessed the power to intercede with gods on behalf of humans. The Egyptians honored these primates with sacrifices and offerings. They believed that these acts could protect them from earthly evils and ensure a safe afterlife.

The belief that baboons were reincarnations of deceased loved ones further elevated their sacred status. Egyptians saw in baboons a reflection of their own society, making them ideal candidates for the embodiment of the human soul. This connection was deepened by the popular belief that baboons could communicate with Ra, the sun god. Their morning rituals of loud calls and stretching postures were interpreted as a form of worship or communication with Ra.

Babi, also known as Baba, simply means the "chief of baboons." Unlike the typical portrayal of gods as benevolent and virtuous, Babi is often depicted as having aggressive and lustful traits. This depiction draws from the nature of baboons, which are known for their aggression and high libido, influencing the perception of Babi as a bloodthirsty deity who lived on the entrails of the unworthy.

In the afterlife, Babi's role was equally significant and daunting.

A common depiction of Babi, who is crouched with an erection.[48]

He was believed to be the devourer of the souls of the unrighteous, similar to another creature known as Ammit (often depicted with the head of a crocodile, the front legs of a lion, and the hindquarters of a hippopotamus). While Ammit often appeared in many Egyptian texts, feared yet respected as the creature that devoured the heart of the unworthy, Babi appeared in other versions of the afterlife journey as an underworld ape god who fed on human entrails and unworthy souls.

His association with virility in the afterlife stems from the high libido observed in baboons. Many depictions of Babi show him with an erect penis, which was seen as a symbol of power and sexual prowess. In some beliefs, this attribute of Babi was thought to serve as a mast for the ferryboat that transported the unrighteous to the underworld, linking him to the journey of the soul after death.

Babi was worshiped most prominently in Hermopolis, known today as El Ashmunein. His worshipers sought his favor for a sexually active afterlife and protection from the horrors of hell. To avoid the wrath of Babi, Egyptians employed spells and magical rituals, particularly in the Hall of Two Truths, where the fate of the soul was determined after death.

The worship of Babi, however, witnessed a significant decline during the reign of Pharaoh Akhenaten, who introduced monotheism with a focus on the worship of the sun god, Amun-Ra. The worship of multiple deities was gradually replaced by the singular worship of Amun-Ra, though the worship of other deities, such as Osiris, Isis, and Horus, was eventually brought back with the rise of Tutankhamun, Akhenaten's son.

Babi's portrayal as a bloodthirsty, virile deity contrasts sharply with the conventional benevolent god figure, offering a glimpse into the Egyptians' great reverence and fear of the natural world. The worship of Babi highlights the intricate relationship between humans, animals, and gods in ancient Egyptian culture.

The Mysterious Medjed

Out of all of the lesser-known deities of the Egyptian pantheon, Medjed stands as one of the most obscure. Mentions of the god first appeared during the New Kingdom, yet his origins remain elusive. Medjed was also mentioned briefly in the Book of the Dead, specifically in the seventeenth chapter. This passage listed various divine beings who resided in the afterlife, so it is safe to assume that Medjed had an important role in the realm of the dead. However, while many other gods of Egypt were listed alongside their own stories and myths and had temples built in their honor, Medjed was the complete opposite. There was no temple or structure erected in dedication to the deity.

However, what truly captured the attention of modern-day people was not just his obscurity but also the way he was depicted and drawn. On a handful of papyri uncovered from the Late Period, Medjed was depicted as a floating figure with a rounded white body. It was as if he was cloaked in a sheet, like a ghost. On his face was only a pair of eyes, and Medjed also had two legs poking out from beneath. The deity had no arms or mouth, only a pair of eyes and feet that looked like sticks. This was indeed a stark contrast compared to the drawings and hieroglyphs of other deities in the pantheon. While figures like Serket, Khnum, and even Seshat were often depicted in a more serious manner, Medjed is seen by modern eyes as more cartoonish. Regardless of his depiction, Medjed might have had a bigger role in the mythical world of Egypt than is commonly thought.

The Book of the Dead, for instance, referred to Medjed as "the smiter." The reason behind this is uncertain. He was believed to have been able to shoot light from his eyes. Some interpret this as Medjed shooting deadly beams of light, similar to eye lasers. There is also a passage in the Book of the Dead that speaks about how Medjed could pass unseen among men. The exact meaning behind this remains a subject of debate. Some scholars suggest Medjed was a symbol of divine justice in its purest, most unpredictable form. His simple, shrouded appearance might reflect his invisibility to the human eye, with his true form hidden beneath a veil.

What we can be sure of is that Medjed was a crucial figure in the afterlife. He was thought to have been a protector of the dead. He was one of the many deities who assisted the souls of the departed with crossing through the various stages of the Du'at. He stood by them, offering guidance and safeguarding souls from any harm imposed by demons.

Medjed recently garnered attention from all over the world. It all began when the Greenfield Papyrus (a document dating from the Third Intermediate Period), which contained a depiction of the minor god, was put on display at the Mori Art Museum in Tokyo and, later, the Fukuoka Museum of Art. Here, a range of Egyptian gods was introduced to a wider audience, but Medjed caught the attention of many. This was largely due to his peculiar depiction. Medjed became an internet sensation in Japan. The Egyptian god was featured in video games and animated shows and even turned into plushies.

In many ways, Medjed's unexpected rise from obscurity to modern pop culture emphasizes the timeless appeal of Egypt's rich mythology. Although Medjed had once been a nearly forgotten figure whose name was mentioned only a handful of times, he now stands as a reminder that even the most mysterious figures can find new life across time and cultures.

Chapter 10: The Impact of Egyptian Mythology on Modern Culture

It is safe to say that the stories and legends of Egypt are not confined only to the ancient past. The compelling narratives of these gods and goddesses, from the most popular ones such as Ra, Set, Isis, and Osiris to the less well-known deities such as Seshat and Babi, and the themes of creation, power, and the underworld have left a lasting imprint that extends far beyond their origins in the sands of Egypt. This final chapter aims to shift our focus from the historical and mythological realms to the contemporary world.

In contemporary literature, the allure of Egyptian mythology has not waned. Modern novels, often seen as gateways to fantasy and adventure, have embraced these ancient narratives, weaving them into stories that resonate with today's readers. A prime example is Rick Riordan's *The Kane Chronicles*, where the rich tapestry of Egyptian myths is brought to life through the eyes of modern characters. Riordan's work blends the ancient and the contemporary, introducing a younger generation to the likes of Osiris, Isis, and Set in a setting they can relate to. This blend of old and new not only entertains but also educates, creating a bridge between the past and the present.

Poetry and plays also find inspiration in Egyptian mythology. They often use mythological references and symbols to explore themes such as life, death, and rebirth. The ancient stories, with their deep philosophical undertones, offer a rich well from which poets and playwrights draw. Whether it's a poem that subtly alludes to the journey of Ra across the sky or a play that centers around the power struggles of the gods, these works bring a piece of ancient Egypt into contemporary literary culture.

The influence of these myths in modern literature is not just about retelling old stories. It is also about reinterpretation and relevance. Contemporary authors and playwrights reinvent these myths, often infusing them with modern themes and perspectives. This reimagining is crucial since it keeps the myths alive, dynamic, and pertinent to current societal contexts.

Of course, the reimagining of Egyptian myths also extends into the visually striking world of film and television. However, compared to the wealth of content inspired by Greek mythology, the foray into Egyptian myths in film and television is relatively less trodden. This scarcity makes the existing works particularly important in keeping the legacy of Egyptian mythology visible in popular culture. Each film or series, by virtue of its rarity, becomes a precious window into the world of ancient Egyptian gods, legends, and lore, invoking curiosity and fascination among audiences.

Blockbuster movies like *The Mummy* series, for example, have played a great role in bringing these ancient tales to a global audience. These films, with their blend of action, adventure, a pinch of comedy, and colorful mythological elements, offer a cinematic interpretation of Egypt's rich mythological history. The portrayal of mummies, curses, and other prominent historical figures in these movies, while often dramatized, has introduced Egyptian mythology to viewers who might never have encountered it otherwise.

Gods of Egypt, with its depiction of the Egyptian gods and goddesses, also provides an intriguing cinematic rendition of one of Egypt's most renowned legends: the epic struggle between Horus and Set. While the film takes creative liberties in its storytelling, such as its unique portrayal of gods and the fantastical elements woven into the narrative, it still helps immortalize these ancient tales.

This reimagining of Horus's journey to reclaim his rightful throne from Set is more than just a tale of good versus evil. It encapsulates the timeless themes of power, justice, and redemption that are central to Egyptian mythology. The film's visualization of these gods, their powers, and the mythical landscapes of ancient Egypt helps to make these ancient stories relatable to a modern audience. Even though the narrative greatly diverges from traditional mythological texts, it succeeds in capturing the essence of the dramatic and complex relationships in the Egyptian pantheon.

As for television, series like Marvel's *Moon Knight* introduce a different flavor to the portrayal of Egyptian mythology. Here, we see a blend of modern storytelling with mythological elements, bringing characters like Khonshu, the Egyptian god of the moon, into a contemporary setting. Documentaries offer a more factual and historical perspective. They usually delve into the archaeological, historical, and cultural aspects of these myths, providing a grounded and educational viewpoint.

Apart from literature and media, the influence of Egyptian mythology also made a resounding impact on the world of architecture and urban design. The Luxor Hotel, an architectural marvel in the heart of Las Vegas, is just one example that stands as a modern homage to the grandeur of ancient Egypt. Its main structure, a colossal pyramid, is an iconic feature on the Las Vegas Strip, complete with a replica of the Sphinx guarding the entrance. The hotel's design goes beyond mere replication; inside, the decor and motifs are infused with elements reminiscent of Egyptian art and mythology, from statues of gods and goddesses to giant sculptures of pharaohs. The blending of ancient symbolism with modern luxury creates an immersive experience, transporting visitors to a bygone era of pharaohs and pyramids.

In a similar vein, Sunway Pyramid in Malaysia is another striking example of Egyptian-inspired architecture. This shopping mall, distinguished by its massive lion-headed Sphinx and a pyramid, is considered a unique landmark in the city of Selangor. The mall's interior, adorned with murals, hieroglyphs, and statues, makes shopping an experience intertwined with cultural exploration.

The Louvre in Paris, renowned for its vast collection of art, features striking glass pyramids in its courtyard and houses an extensive collection of ancient Egyptian artifacts. The modern glass pyramids outside give a modern twist to the classic museum building, creating a visual dialogue between the old and the new, the ancient and the modern. Inside, visitors can experience firsthand the art, culture, and rich mythology of ancient Egypt. This space in the Louvre serves as both a tribute and a bridge, connecting contemporary viewers to the distant past of the Egyptian civilization.

In addition to architectural landmarks in various countries, Egyptian motifs have also found their way into public art and spaces, further illustrating the pervasive influence of this ancient civilization. For instance, in several metropolitan areas, one might encounter sculptures or murals depicting Egyptian deities or symbols like the Eye of Horus, an ancient Egyptian symbol of protection, royal power, and good health. There might even be representations of pharaonic iconography. These pieces of art, whether in the form of a standalone sculpture in a park or a detailed mural on a city wall, bring a touch of ancient mystique to modern public spaces. They serve as visual reminders of the enduring legacy of Egyptian culture and its capacity to inspire artists across generations and regions.

These symbols from Egyptian mythology are part of our daily lives, often without us even realizing it. The ankh, known as the key of life, is frequently seen in various forms of jewelry, fashion, and even in popular media, symbolizing life and immortality.

While direct phrases and references from Egyptian mythology are less common in everyday language compared to visual symbols, the impact of these myths is still evident in various cultural references. For instance, terms like "pharaoh" are often used metaphorically to represent power and authority, and references to mummies and pyramids are commonly found in popular culture.

Modern artists often draw inspiration from the rich iconography and symbolism of ancient Egypt, creating works that fuse the old and the new. These artistic endeavors range from paintings and sculptures to digital art, echoing the motifs, color schemes, and narrative elements of Egyptian mythology. For instance, artists like Judy Chicago and Ellen Gallagher have incorporated elements of Egyptian mythology in their works.

The influence of Egyptian mythology is equally striking in the world of fashion. Designers have long been fascinated by the opulence and mystique of ancient Egypt, which is often reflected in collections featuring bold prints, hieroglyphic patterns, and accessories reminiscent of Egyptian art. For instance, fashion shows have seen models adorned with Cleopatra-style headpieces and jewelry or garments that echo the regal draping of pharaonic clothing. These fashion statements are more than just a nod to historical aesthetics; they are also a modern reinterpretation of the mythological and cultural richness of Egypt.

In this journey through the echoes of Egyptian mythology in our modern world, we have seen how these ancient narratives continue to weave their magic into various aspects of contemporary culture. From the imaginative retellings in literature and the captivating representations in film and television to the architectural wonders inspired by ancient structures, these age-old stories maintain a vibrant presence. The symbols and expressions derived from these myths enrich our daily lives, and the artistic and fashion industries continue to draw inspiration from the rich Egyptian culture.

The enduring legacy of Egyptian mythology lies in its timeless appeal and the universal themes it explores. Of course, not all the stories of gods and pharaohs survived the test of time, but those that did resonate with such universality and depth that they continue to captivate us today.

Conclusion

This exploration into the pantheon of Egyptian gods and goddesses has been more than an excursion into the past; it has also been a journey into the heart of human experience, revealing enduring themes and universal truths that resonate through time. It is safe to say that as we close the final pages of this journey, we find ourselves not at the end but rather at the beginning of a deeper understanding.

True, these gods and goddesses are no longer worshiped. In fact, even the grandest of their temples left to us are only in ruins, with some others probably still buried deep in the golden sands. Nevertheless, the narratives involving these deities continue to speak to us, highlighting the enduring relevance of ancient wisdom in our contemporary world.

The Egyptians saw the divine in almost everything, from the grandeur of the pyramids to the simplicity of the Nile's ebb and flow. This sense of interconnectedness—the belief that every element of the world is part of a greater whole—is a powerful reminder of our own connection to the universe and to each other. In our modern times, where the threat of environmental degradation looms large, this ancient worldview urges us to reconsider our relationship with nature and the importance of living in harmony with our environment.

The societal structures and spiritual practices of ancient Egypt also offer timeless lessons in governance, justice, and morality. The Egyptians' emphasis on Ma'at (the concept of truth, balance, and order) in their daily lives and in their governance clearly proved their advanced societal organization and their deep understanding of ethical living. In our world of complex social and political challenges, the Egyptian commitment to balance and harmony presents a model for creating more equitable and just societies. They remind us that leadership should be balanced with compassion, that justice requires fairness, and that our actions always have consequences.

The legends of the Egyptian gods and goddesses still speak to us today because of how they address fundamental human concerns: the mysteries of life and death, the quest for knowledge and power, the need for protection, and the search for meaning. The tales of deities like Ra, Osiris, Isis, Set, Horus, and even Serket or Thoth continue to offer comfort and guidance in our search for understanding in the face of life's uncertainties.

These myths also speak to the power of imagination and storytelling in shaping our understanding of the world and universe. They are not just wild stories where logic and science take a back seat. Yes, these legends are infused with exaggerations and creativity, but within their fantastical elements lie wisdom, truths, and insights. In these tales, the gods and mythical beings do more than just go on adventures. Their journeys also gave way for us to think and wonder.

These myths are indeed a testament to the resilience and adaptability of human cultures. They have transcended time and geography, finding relevance in different eras and societies. The ancient Egyptians might have lived in a world vastly different from ours, but their stories continue to inspire, educate, and resonate with people across the world today.

Part 2: Pharaohs of Ancient Egypt

An Enthralling Overview of Egyptian Rulers

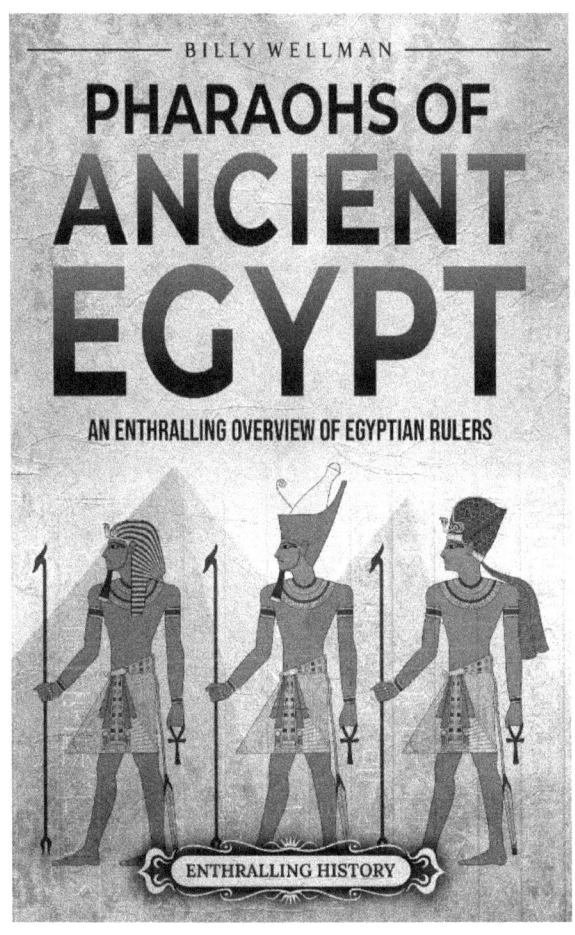

Introduction

Ancient Egypt is fascinating. It was such a different world from ours, so distant in time, with such spectacular monuments. Learning about its history can be overwhelming. Some academic Egyptologists remember looking at the great Tutankhamun exhibition in the 1970s and being drawn into what would eventually become a lifetime of involvement. Kent Weeks, excavator of the largest tomb in the Valley of the Kings, remembers when he decided on a career in Egyptology; he was only eight years old.

It is easy to see ancient Egypt as one homogeneous mass. But in fact, when Ramesses II looked at the pyramids of Giza, he was looking way back in time, like us today looking at the Vikings or the earliest Pueblo peoples. The ancient Egyptian civilization lasted for over three thousand years, and ancient Egyptians were well aware of it. Kings who came to power in difficult times often tried to press the reset button by invoking earlier great pharaohs.

The sources for Egyptian history are difficult to interpret, particularly in the earliest times. For instance, we have different king lists containing nearly two hundred different names, and they do not all agree with each other. Some of the pharaohs mentioned in the lists are just names, while others are individuals about whom we have a huge amount of both archaeological and written information. Pharaohs like Seti I, who had king lists carved into their temples, often skipped the pharaohs they disapproved of, so there are blanks we have to fill.

In some cases, there are blanks because parts of the historical texts have been destroyed. For instance, the Palermo Stone, which was inscribed with the royal annals of the first five dynasties, exists only in fragments; a huge amount of the original record is missing. The Turin King List or the Turin Royal Canon, a papyrus dating from the New Kingdom, is also fragmentary. Even with the extra pieces that were discovered in 2009, it is still only about half complete.

Pharaohs had five different official names, so sometimes what looks like two pharaohs might be just one (such as Djoser and Netjerikhet, for instance). And when Greek historians wrote down what they thought they had heard, they often got it wrong. For example, Khufu became Cheops, Djoser became Sesorthos, and Ramesses II became Ozymandias (from his throne name Usermaatre Setepenre). That makes reconciling Greek and Egyptian written sources tricky.

It is also difficult to get behind the ideological filters that pharaohs applied in their public pronouncements and imagery. When we look at an image of Ramesses II, are we looking at him as he was or as he wanted people to think of him?

Fortunately, we do have some other sources that can get us closer to the pharaohs. In some cases, we can actually see the real man—or at least his mummified body. With modern investigative techniques, we can read a mummy like a book. (It is fascinating just how many of the great pharaohs suffered from arthritis and how bad their teeth were.) In other cases, we have accounts of their actions written by officials, accounts from their palaces, or even diplomatic correspondence.

One thing that is very evident is that the pharaohs made ancient Egypt different from other civilizations. The concept of a divine king led to the establishment of a centralized economy and bureaucracy. Through the dynastic progression, Egypt sought stability. While it didn't always get it, the fact that regicide occurred only twice in 2,800 years (Ramesses III and Amenemhet I) is quite amazing, compared to the turnover in kings of Israel, or Hittite or Persian kings.[i]

It's also notable that when foreign rulers managed to take over Egypt, they straightaway started to present themselves as pharaohs, taking Egyptian throne names and showing themselves performing the pharaonic

---

[i] It is possible that regicide occurred more often in ancient Egypt. Since their deaths occurred thousands and thousands of years ago, it is hard to know for sure how the pharaohs met their end.

rituals dressed in the kilt and wearing the double crown of the king of the Two Lands. The Egyptian culture was so strong that when the Nubians invaded from the south, they did so because they had come to believe they preserved a purer version of the Egyptian religion than the Egyptians!

This book will shine a new light on the pharaohs, including explaining how the concept of divine kingship began to emerge in the pre-dynastic period. It will tell the stories of those pharaohs whose reigns and works are the most interesting and intriguing, and it will also look at what remains of their legacy. You don't need to know anything about archaeology or Egyptology; everything you need to know will be explained to you. By the time you come to the end of this book, you should have a good grasp of how ancient Egypt developed over time, and you'll have some fascinating stories to tell your friends and family.

Chapter 1: Early Pharaohs: The First Dynastic Period

The story of the pharaohs doesn't start with the first pharaoh. It starts a good deal further back than that.

In the last fifty years or so, archaeologists have discovered a great deal about Egypt's pre-dynastic history. Evidence shows that the idea of kingship was gradually developing even before the first king of Egypt took the throne.

For most of us, the earliest recognizable monuments of ancient Egypt are the pyramids. However, the beginnings of the pyramid builders' culture went back five hundred years. During the pre-dynastic period and the first couple of dynasties, Egypt created the foundations of its distinctive civilization and culture.

Egypt's prehistoric cultures suddenly made a big advance during the Naqada II period (c. 3600-3150 BCE). Technology improved; for instance, pottery moved from handmade ware using alluvial clay (found on the surface) to mass production using marl clay, which had to be dug out. They also used a higher firing temperature, which made it stronger. Egypt became more u. While earlier periods show distinct local cultures, the material culture of different sites became much more cohesive in the late Naqada period.

At the same time, grave goods became much more elaborate, and the distinction between the graves of the wealthy and the commoners became greater. A wealthy class was beginning to distinguish itself from the rest of the people, leading to social stratification. Populations became denser, and small city-states arose along the Nile. Three of them eventually became predominant: Naqada (about twelve miles north of today's Luxor), Thinis (likely today's Abydos), and Nekhen/Hierakonpolis (over one hundred miles north of modern Aswan).

At some point, Egypt developed an ideology of kingship. It had already been fully formed by the time of the First Dynasty. By that time, Egypt had not just a pharaoh but also a civil service, writing, and monumental architecture. Almost everything in later Egypt had its roots in these first few centuries. But how soon can we identify "kingship?"

At Abydos, excavations discovered a huge pre-dynastic cemetery full of elite tombs. Tomb U-j in the Umm el-Qa'ab cemetery is a multi-chambered tomb that includes rooms for the storage of several thousand liters of wine and even bone labels with writing on them (though it's difficult to read the symbols with any certainty). It appears that the wine came from many different towns, some in the Nile Delta. Either Egypt was already under one ruler, or whoever was buried in Tomb U-j was rich enough to trade with the other areas. The tomb also contains some artifacts imported from Syria.

Tomb U-j contains one particularly interesting artifact: a heka scepter, which is one of the pharaoh's regalia. We don't know who was buried in the tomb, though some Egyptologists have identified him as a pre-dynastic "king," Scorpion I. Whoever he was, he certainly had some kind of royal status.

Other pre-dynastic finds show the development of kingly iconography. For instance, the Abydos Vessel found in Cemetery U shows a man smiting his enemy with a mace; this became the stereotypical kingly posture of later dynasties. Cloth from a tomb at Gebelein shows a hippopotamus being harpooned, a symbol of triumph over the wild and chaos, which became another pharaonic motif.

The "master of the beasts" motif, which is found in a painted tomb in Hierakonpolis, was borrowed from Mesopotamia. The idea is similar to the hippo-harpooning scene, showing a man throttling two animals, one on each side. However, this foreign motif didn't stand the test of time, as the Egyptians soon stopped using it.

Cemetery U at Abydos contains the tombs of the pharaohs of the First Dynasty, as well as two kings of what has been termed "Dynasty 0." These two kings, Iry-Hor and Ka, aren't found in the official king lists. So, it seems that whoever is buried in Tomb U-j had established the site as a place for royal entombment. Therefore, whatever his name might have been, he must have been a king.

Under pre-dynastic kings like Ka and Scorpion II, the process of state formation advanced further. For instance, Ka is buried at Abydos, but artifacts bearing his name are found as far afield as Helwan (near Cairo), Wadi Tumilat (east of the Nile Delta), and as far north as Israel (Tel Lod). His name is found with signs that refer to treasury revenue, so we can assume that the economy was centralized. This most likely began with the state taking control of the agricultural surplus so that central granaries could provide a form of insurance policy against drought.

Scorpion II is known from the scorpion mace head found in a temple at Hierakonpolis, which appears to date back to the late pre-dynastic period. It shows a figure wearing the white crown or hedjet of Upper Egypt, the tall conical crown with a bulbous finial. The figure is holding a hoe and is attended by servants; he is perhaps performing an irrigation rite, opening a dike, or sowing seed, and he is accompanied by fan bearers. His name, like Ka's, is attested by ivory tags and stone and clay vessels with the royal serekh mark, a rectangular enclosure representing a niched palace façade.

The first king of Egypt who is recognized in the Egyptian king lists is Narmer, who was probably the successor of Scorpion II. However, some Egyptologists believe he may have been the

An example of a Horus serekh.[48]

same person as Scorpion. (If you want to see how he belongs to the predynastic world, just think of him as "King Catfish," the first hieroglyph of his name.) Narmer was probably also the same king as Menes, who was identified as the first king of a united Egypt by Manetho, the late Egyptian scholar who wrote a history of Egypt and created the method of dividing Egyptian history into dynasties. This system is still used today.

Narmer became king sometime around 3000 BCE. At Hierakonpolis, he dedicated the Narmer Palette, a stone palette. Egyptians used palettes for grinding cosmetics, but the Narmer Palette was much bigger; it was over two feet tall. Both sides are carved. On one side, Narmer wears the white crown, and on the other, he wears the red crown (deshret) of Lower Egypt. The mastery of stone carving displayed in this work is evidence of a high level of material culture.

The two sides of the Narmer Palette."

The palette shows Narmer as a remarkably brutal king. He is shown striking his enemy with a mace while grabbing him by the hair; this became a stereotypical image of the conquering pharaoh for the next three thousand years. Decapitated prisoners are shown lying in rows, placed with their heads between their legs. A bull appears on one side of the palette, and the human Narmer wears a bull's tail to show his bull-like power. The bull's tail and names such as "Victorious Bull" appear throughout Egyptian history. Narmer is also clearly associated with the falcon, the emblem of the god Horus.

The falcon sits on top of the serekh. As we mentioned already, a serekh is a rectangular enclosure representing a niched palace façade, in which the king's name is usually written. Later, the serekh became the cartouche, but both the serekh and cartouche were (with a few exceptions) reserved for the king.

Because Narmer is shown wearing both crowns, he is undeniably claiming kingship of both halves of Egypt. But does the palette show a historical fact, making Narmer the conqueror and unifier of the two lands, or is it simply a ritual artifact showing his status as the wearer of the double crown? We don't know for sure. However, in early coronation rituals, "Unification of the Two Lands" was one of the rites, which is evidence that it was, in fact, a ritual artifact.

Narmer was buried at Abydos next to the tombs of Ka and his successor, Hor-Aha.

Hor-Aha's tomb is larger than those of Ka and Narmer. It has three separate chambers, which would have been covered by a wooden roof after the king's burial, and a mound built over the top. Then, two stelae (large rock markers) would have been placed on the mound. This would have been a common pattern for the tombs at Abydos, but Hor-Aha added a new twist. His tomb is at the center of thirty-six separate subsidiary burials, including servants, women, dogs, and lions. None of the members of his court buried around his tomb were much older than twenty-five, suggesting they were killed at the time of Hor-Aha's burial to accompany him into the next life. The practice of retainer sacrifices continued with the remaining tombs of the First Dynasty.

The earliest elite tombs at Saqqara, in the desert near Cairo, date from Hor-Aha's reign and suggest that he had chosen nearby Memphis as his capital, although he continued the tradition of interment at Abydos. An ivory box found at Abydos bears his name along with that of Benerib, "sweet of heart," who was perhaps one of his wives. Another of his wives was Khenthap, who was the mother of Hor-Aha's successor, Djer.

Most importantly, the systematic keeping of annals first appeared during Hor-Aha's reign, marking the beginning of Egyptian history. This was the moment at which Egypt became conscious of having a past.[1] An entry on the Palermo Stone, a record of activities overseen by each pharaoh, shows that Hor-Aha carried out a royal progress known as the

---

[1] Wilkinson, Toby A. H. *Early Dynastic Egypt.* Routledge, London, 1999. Pg. 2.

"Following of Horus," which reasserted royal authority along the Nile. It also could have been a tax-gathering expedition. (Beginning in the Second Dynasty, the Following of Horus was combined with a formal census.)

The name of Horus is important, as it shows that the royal myth of the sun god Ra (or Re; we're not quite sure how Egyptians pronounced their language, so the pronunciation changed over time) and his son Horus was already in place. Ra was the original king of Egypt. He sent his son, the falcon-headed Horus, to rule the land. Each pharaoh was thought to be the incarnation of Horus, so the pharaoh's first kingly name was his Horus name.

Each pharaoh was seen as a god and as the son of a god. When the pharaoh died, he passed to the west, which was seen as the land of the setting sun. From very early times, Abydos was seen as a sacred land and the home of Khenti-Amentiu, the lord of the westerners and the god of the land of the dead; that is why it was chosen as the first royal necropolis.

The Geography of Egypt

To understand Egypt, the central place of the Nile has to be recognized. Ancient Egypt was a long, thin nation, running along the banks of the Nile. To the ancient Egyptians, the Nile was known simply as *iteru*, meaning "great river." Every year, the river overflowed its banks (the "inundation"), bringing silt as well as water to the land and making the flood plain fertile. This allowed the establishment of settled communities and the creation of an agricultural surplus.

The fertile Nile Valley was surrounded by desert and mountains. It was relatively inaccessible to other powers in the Middle East, so it was easy to secure against invaders. Easy boat travel along the river enabled the centralization of the state and the spread of a homogeneous culture. This gave Egypt a different history from the civilizations of Mesopotamia and the Levant, which saw waves of kingdoms and empires competing for dominance.

However, Egypt has two different types of geography. In the south, the Nile ran in a fertile flood plain between desert cliffs; in the north, it spread out into a delta, which was often marshy and wild. The papyrus, a marsh plant, was the symbol of Lower Egypt (the northern delta), while the lotus or lily stood for Upper Egypt (the southern valley). Even though

Egypt was unified as early as 3000 BCE, the two parts of Egypt were always recognized separately. The pharaoh was the king of Two Lands.

An interesting note: Egyptians orientated themselves toward the south. An Egyptian map of Egypt would have had Aswan at the top and the delta at the bottom, following the direction of the Nile from its origins to the sea.

Djer was the first pharaoh to take a full Golden Horus name. His full title was Djer Ny-nebu Iteti, "the defender of Horus, who belongs to the golden one, the ruler." He probably came to the throne as a child, as his reign was preceded by a regency under Neithhotep, who might have been his mother or grandmother.

Neithhotep was buried in a huge tomb surrounded by niched walls at Naqada, and her name is sometimes written in a serekh, suggesting that she ruled on her own. The niched palace wall created a corrugated outline that must have been very striking when it was new. It was borrowed from Mesopotamian architecture, and it was the only theme from foreign art that remained influential after the first few kings. It appears in Djoser's tomb complex, which was created at the start of the Old Kingdom.

Djer built his tomb at Abydos, and it was surrounded by 325 subsidiary graves. He was the first to build an enclosure separate from the tomb. The tombs of the First Dynasty kings at Abydos included food, wine, other artifacts, servants, and even donkeys and boats, all of which were provided for the king to use in his future life. The provisions found in the enclosures appear to be more generally for the royal household, while those in the tomb were specifically for the king. The enclosure copied the exterior of a palace and provided everything the king needed to carry out the rites and ceremonies of kingship. The tomb, on the other hand, was created as a palace interior and included everything the king would need for his daily life.

Each enclosure appears to have been destroyed by the builder of the next; this may have been a symbolic "burying" of the enclosure to make it available to its owner in the afterlife. The tomb was also "buried" twice, first under a mound that was built over the top of the wooden-roofed tomb chambers, and then the mound itself was buried under more earth. The mound might have been a reflection of the primeval mound, which the Egyptians believed was the place of creation, the first place to become separate from the chaotic waters.

It is quite likely that each enclosure was used for the royal cult during the king's lifetime rather than being just a funerary monument. It is also likely that the enclosure began the process of developing a royal style of architecture: the high niched wall. It is also worth noting that the words "sacred" and "set apart" are the same word in ancient Egyptian, and exclusion was a principle of Egyptian culture from a very early date. For instance, temples developed as a series of more and more exclusive spaces, using gateways to close off each stage of the approach. Ancient Egypt is all about secrets within secrets, which is one reason why it is so fascinating to learn about!

Djer's tomb was re-roofed in the Middle Kingdom as the tomb of Osiris, a god who did not appear in the records until the Fifth Dynasty. Records of the nilometer measures for the Nile's inundation exist from Djer's reign, showing that Egypt already had the ability to methodically measure the height of the waters. Since farmers were taxed according to their theoretical harvest, which was calculated on the area they farmed and the nilometer reading for the year, this wasn't just a meteorological or agricultural statistic; it was also the basis for Egypt's tax system.

Djet, "Serpent of Horus," succeeded Djer, but he did not have a long reign. The records of his reign have been lost from the Palermo Stone. Vessel seals showing his name prove that Egypt traded actively to the north in Syria and Canaan. Djet's tomb was surrounded by 174 subsidiary burials and was topped by a stela showing his Horus name, which can now be seen in the Louvre Museum in Paris, France. Also found in the tomb were an ivory comb with his name on it and a number of copper tools.

The stelae of Djet, showing his serekh. The Horus falcon is on top, his name, "Serpent," is in the middle, and at the bottom is a representation of the niched façade of a royal palace. "

All the tombs at Abydos were robbed of their more valuable contents at some point, but the fragments and overlooked or less valuable pieces have shown the sophistication of Egyptian art and craft even at this early date.

Merneith was most likely Djer's daughter. She was the mother of Den, the next pharaoh. As such, it's likely that she was Djet's senior royal wife. Djet was probably her brother or half-brother.

Merneith was buried in the royal cemetery at Abydos, so it appears likely that she ruled on her own when Den was too young to exercise power. Her tomb was surrounded by forty subsidiary burials, which is, again, likely to be a sign of her kingly status. A seal found in Den's tomb lists the Horus names of the kings. Merneith has the title of "King's Mother," and her name is shown in a serekh on a seal found in Saqqara.

Merneith had a second tomb in Saqqara, near modern Cairo. The creation of two tombs often occurred, as it allowed pharaohs to have their bodies buried in one place while maintaining their claim to eternal life in another place as well. (Later on, Seti I would have his tomb built in the Valley of the Kings. He also built a cenotaph (an empty tomb), now known as the Osireion, which was attached to his mortuary temple in Abydos.)

Whether or not Neithhotep and Merneith were regarded as pharaohs in their own right, it is certain that royal women were respected and powerful in the First Dynasty.

Den was the son of Merneith and Djet. He was the first to use the title *Nsw-bity*, "he of the sedge and bee," which is usually interpreted as king of both Upper and Lower Egypt but may also reflect a new conception of the king as both divine and human. The new title stresses the king's role in binding the country together and maintaining harmony in the cosmos. He was also the first to be shown wearing the double crown—that is, wearing the white crown inside the red crown rather than wearing each separately.

Den's tomb includes what we can treat as a First Dynasty king list. The tomb has seal impressions forming a list of Den's predecessors from Narmer onward. It includes Merneith but not Neithhotep. His tomb also includes ebony and ivory tags that show him running with the Apis bull and celebrating two Sed festivals (jubilees). Den was the first to build a staircase down to his tomb, which meant the tomb could be completed before his burial since it could be fully roofed. Previously, the roof was built over the chamber after the burial had been performed. This was also the first tomb to use stone; earlier tombs only used mudbricks. The tomb was paved with red and black granite brought down the Nile from Aswan.

Den made a census of the population and reorganized lands in the Nile Delta, possibly redesignating them as crown lands. He appears to have increased the resources of the administration and carried out a reform of the administration, with new titles of officials including the word "controller." He also set up the "White House," though this meant the treasury department for the ancient Egyptians, not his official residence.

The earliest papyrus ever found can be dated to Den's reign. Hemaka, Den's chancellor, built himself a luxurious tomb at Saqqara. Just in case he needed to write things down in the next life, his tomb included a box full of unused papyrus sheets, among other grave goods.

The number of elite tombs at Saqqara during Den's reign was greater than that of any other First or Second Dynasty king. That can partly be attributed to his long reign, which probably lasted over forty years. It also shows how the number of administrators grew quickly. Over one hundred subsidiary burials surround Den's tomb.

Den was succeeded by Anedjib, Semerkhet, and Qa'a, the last king of the First Dynasty. It's interesting that the subsidiary burials around Qa'a's tomb numbered only twenty-six; ritual sacrifices were going out of fashion by that point. Perhaps ideas of how the pharaoh would reach the afterlife and what he would do there were changing.

Hotepsekhemwy was the first ruler of the Second Dynasty. There might have been one or two short-lived claimants (such as Horus Bird, though that might be an alternative name used by Qa'a, and Sneferka) before Hotepsekhemwy was able to take the throne. The new pharaoh's Horus name may indicate that he felt there was a need for reconciliation since it means "Reconciliation of the Two Powers." Perhaps Upper and Lower Egypt had been split during the intervening period.

Hotepsekhemwy made one move that was unexpected; he decided to place the royal tombs at Saqqara. He ignored the elite tombs that clustered to the north of Saqqara and created an exclusively royal burial site. His tomb, which he appears to have shared with his son Raneb, was the first to have a portcullis of limestone. In fact, it has four. These were slotted into place to close the tomb once the pharaoh had been interred. A staircase leads down to a main gallery from which storage chambers branch off to both sides. There are more than eighty separate spaces.

The mastaba (a type of tomb with a flat top and sloping sides) developed from the rounded mound of the Abydos-style tomb. Perhaps it was a way of evoking the impressive outline of the royal enclosures at Abydos. While the burial chamber itself was reached by a deep shaft, on the surface, there was a rectangular, flat-topped superstructure with inward-sloping sides. The mastaba contained a chapel with a false door where offerings could be made to the *ka*, or the spirit, of the deceased.

A number of kings followed Hotepsekhemwy, and they likely were buried at Saqqara. However, Pharaoh Seth-Peribsen appeared to have held some sort of one-king revolution. He did two unusual things. First, he named himself Seth-Peribsen, using an animal to honor Seth (a jackal-like creature) rather than a falcon on top of his serekh. Seth was Horus's enemy, so this was an odd move. Seth-Peribsen also decided to build his tomb in Abydos, turning his back on the newly established tradition of using Saqqara as the royal cemetery. While he erected an enclosure, he did not go back to the practice of ritual sacrifice.

There are various theories about why Seth-Peribsen did this. He might have inherited only half of the realm from the previous pharaoh, Nynetjer; so far, his name has not been found anywhere in Lower Egypt, which might have been under a separate ruler. His name is also missing from the "official" king lists. Regardless, he seemed to have been something of a live wire, reforming the bureaucracy and ensuring it had a clearly defined hierarchical structure.

The last king of the Second Dynasty was Khasekhem, who took the throne after a period in which the king lists are somewhat confused. His Horus name means "the power has appeared," which would have been a good name for a pharaoh who aimed to revive the country after a period of conflict and turmoil. He later changed his name by adding a plural to Khasekhemwy ("the powerful ones have appeared") and adding a Seth animal as well as a Horus animal above his serekh. Perhaps this was part of his attempt to reunify Egypt after whatever had happened with Seth-Peribsen.

Khasekhemwy was one of the most prolific builders of the early period. He appears to have reigned for nearly twenty years, which gave him enough time to construct a number of impressive buildings. At Abydos, he built both a tomb and a huge mudbrick enclosure, which still stands today. It is known as the Shunet El Zebib or "raisin barn." The niches on its walls are still visible, imitating a palace façade like the one shown on the serekh. In the very middle of the otherwise empty courtyard, Egyptologist David O'Connor discovered a square of rubble and brick that formed four steps. It's impossible to be certain about it, but it has been suggested that the structure could be a proto-pyramid, the very first step in the design process that would eventually lead to Khufu's immense pyramid in iaza.

Another feature that is associated with Khasekhemwy's enclosure is fourteen boat burials. The boats were not only buried but also lined with mudbricks. While the meaning here is uncertain, boats appear in Khufu's pyramid, where they have a very specific meaning. Again, Khasekhemwy seemed to have anticipated later developments with uncanny accuracy.

Khasekhemwy's tomb in the royal cemetery was the first to be built in dressed quarried stones, and it contained some glorious craftsmanship, including a carnelian scepter dressed with bands of gold, a bronze basin, and stone vases with gold-leaf lids. There were also flint and copper tools and carnelian beads.

He built a huge niched palace façade enclosure at Hierakonpolis, and he might have built the huge Gisr el-Mudir enclosure at Saqqara too (three separate enclosures in three of the most important places in Egypt during his time). Perhaps he felt that as the pharaoh who was trying to reunify Egypt, he needed to be seen as "present" in all these places. He also needed to know what was going on, and according to the Palermo Stone, he carried out "a census of gold and fields" to assess the nation's financial and agricultural resources.

A beautifully carved statue of Khasekhemwy from the Hierakonpolis temple enclosure shows him seated, wearing the tight, long-sleeved robe that pharaohs typically wore at their Sed festival. One hand had been drilled to hold a scepter, and he wears the white crown. On the plinth is a record of a military campaign and depicts the contorted bodies of Khasekhemwy's enemies. A label reads "47,209 northern enemies." That's a stunningly precise number; if it's true, his civil service must have been working overtime.

Khasekhemwy was succeeded by his son Djoser, which shows that he had laid a secure foundation for the dynastic succession. However, Manetho decided that Djoser was such an important figure that he deserved to start a new dynasty. Djoser's reign started the Old Kingdom, so we will start with his reign in the next chapter.

By the end of the Second Dynasty, ancient Egypt was recognizably the ancient Egypt as we think of it, though without the pyramids. The image of the pharaoh as the preserver of order and the idea of building funerary monuments had been established. The people saw the pharaoh as semi-divine. The image of Den standing in a skiff and harpooning a hippo, the emblem of the wild marshes and of evil, is repeated more than 1,500 years later in the gilded statuettes of Tutankhamun standing on his skiff with a spear in hand (admittedly without a hippopotamus in sight).

The association of Horus with the pharaoh is evident by the end of the Second Dynasty as well. The scepter and the crook became so iconic that it was used as the hieroglyph meaning "ruler." The flail was also found at an early date, and the classical combination of a crook and flail was first seen in the Second Dynasty. The pharaoh already wore the red and white crowns, separately, as well as the dual crown.

Many of Egypt's gods had long been established by the end of the Second Dynasty. For instance, there was the jackal Anubis, the lord of the dead; the fertility god Min; and the creator god Ptah. However, some deities had yet to be created. There is no evidence that the cow-headed goddess Hathor was around at this point, though a cow goddess called Bat existed. Several animal gods that were known during the early centuries of ancient Egypt but became less well known include Heqet, the frog goddess; Hedjwer, the baboon god; and Harsaphes, the ram. Horus, obviously, was one of the most important gods; in this period, he appeared to have been more important than Ra, though this would soon change.

The two gods who are not found in the early period and who became supremely important later on are Isis and Osiris. Isis does not appear at all. At Abydos, Khenti-Amentiu was worshiped as the lord of the dead; later, he would be merged into the figure of Osiris.

Astronomy was already advanced enough to predict the date of the Nile inundation, and records of the nilometer measures were kept. By the beginning of the Old Kingdom, Egypt already had a centralized economy, which could fund the pharaohs' temple and tomb building projects and was able to guarantee emergency stores of food in the state's granaries. The ancient Egyptian words for "scribe" and "functionary" began to be used in the Second Dynasty. This administration would stay virtually unchanged for the next three thousand years.

Royal estates were created to support each pharaoh's cult after his death. Many of these remained in existence for several dynasties. Djoser's "Horus, foremost star of the sky" estate was still working in the Nineteenth Dynasty, 1,400 years after Djoser died.[1] This helped to centralize agricultural land in royal hands. The early centralization of the economy was probably one reason Egypt didn't develop coinage until very late in its history.

The oil presses, vineyards, pig farms, and even linen weaving, bread making, and brewing were centrally controlled. The standard diet was bread and beer, even at court. Meat was a rare treat except for the ruling class. Craft specializations and increasing social stratification meant people

---

[1] Wilkinson, Toby A. H. *Early Dynastic Egypt.* Pg. 103.

were no longer tied to the land and allowed for the creation of Egypt's earliest towns. Early towns included Elephantine, Hierakonpolis, Memphis, and Naqada. The buildings were built of mudbricks and, in some cases, surrounded by mudbrick walls. At Elephantine, a huge fort was built to protect the southern entry point to the Nile Valley and operate as a customs center for goods brought from the south.

By the end of the first two dynasties, the system of dividing the country into forty-two nomes, each headed by a nomarch, had been created, as had the phyle system of rotation, an effective way of managing human resources. Effectively, ancient Egypt had job sharing, so a man might have been a priest for part of the time and a craftsman for the rest of it.

Chapter 2: The Pharaohs of the Old Kingdom

We don't know much about even the best attested pharaohs of the first two dynasties, but this changes dramatically with the first king of the Third Dynasty, Djoser/Netjerikhet, and the beginning of the Old Kingdom.

Djoser was the son of Khasekhemwy and his great royal wife, Nimaathap. It's not quite clear whether he succeeded his father directly. Many king lists have a pharaoh named Nebka before Djoser, but this name is difficult to reconcile with the Horus names of the kings. The seals on Khasekhemwy's tomb name Djoser but not Nebka. Djoser took the Horus name Netjerikhet, "divine of body," unambiguously asserting his status as both king and god.

Djoser might have married his half-sister, as his wife Hetephernebti retained the title of "King's Daughter." She was likely a child of Khasekhemwy, just like Djoser.

Sibling marriage played an important role in the Egyptian kingdom. It was reserved only for the pharaoh, as was the keeping of a harem. Ordinary Egyptians had one wife. It could be a cousin but certainly never a sister.

The practice of royal sister-brother marriage emphasized the difference between the pharaoh and his subjects. It also related him to the gods. One of the main Egyptian creation myths (there were several) tells how the gods were born from several generations of sister-brother mating (Shu and Tefnut, Nut and Geb, Osiris and Isis, and Seth and Nephthys).

This marriage also had the pragmatic result of keeping the number of grandchildren low, reducing the chances of a contested succession. (Royal women generally could not marry commoners, though this rule was enforced with various degrees of severity at different times. Royal women were never married abroad, though the pharaoh often took foreign wives.) At the same time, since a son by a minor wife could become a pharaoh, polygamy reduced the likelihood of a pharaoh having no heir at all.

Memphis (now on the outskirts of Cairo) became the capital of Egypt. Its Egyptian name was "White Walls," Inebu-hedj; its mudbrick walls were perhaps whitewashed and must have dazzled the eye. Here, Djoser ruled for perhaps twenty or even twenty-eight years. His reign was not the longest in Egyptian history by any means, but it was one of the most important. He is also the first king to be shown in the nemes headdress, a striped cloth with two lappets falling on each side. You may not think it sounds familiar, but you likely know it. Tutankhamun's golden mask shows him wearing the nemes. The colossi that line the façade of Abu Simbel wear the nemes together with the double crown.

The golden mask of King Tut. [46]

We know the names of Djoser's officials, most of whom were buried in Saqqara. For instance, Hesy-Ra, "confidant of the king," had an elegant tomb with mural paintings in vivid colors and beautifully carved cedar panels showing him at different stages of his life. He also might have been Djoser's dentist, depending on the interpretation of one of his titles, which could mean "ivory worker" or "tooth healer." Khabausokar, also "confidant of the king," shows himself in his tomb wearing a leopard-skin kilt and was nicknamed "the Jerboa," a hopping desert rodent.

And then there was Imhotep, the vizier (which could probably be translated as "prime minister" or "chancellor"). Imhotep had the great responsibility of designing and creating Djoser's funerary monument, the first of the great pyramids of Egypt.

Djoser certainly would have known Khasekhemwy's tomb and enclosure, and he appears to have developed the idea further. A huge enclosure with niched palace walls was designed to include the mastaba at the center of the courtyard. Rather than separating the tomb and the enclosure, as was the case at Abydos, Djoser decided to put one within the other. The use of stone columns, carved to resemble the papyrus columns that would have been used in vernacular buildings of the time, and the creation of a closed colonnade were also innovations.

Excavations have shown that Djoser originally planned a great mastaba tomb in the middle of the enclosure. Later, a four-stepped pyramid was planned, but this was increased in size to the six-stepped pyramid that exists today. It is fascinating to see how the design evolved as Djoser and Imhotep gained confidence; the whole complex has been called a "staggering achievement," going far beyond anything that had been built by that point.[i]

The compound includes several features that are still not completely understood. For instance, while the main tomb is under the pyramid, there is a south tomb that may have housed the king's ka statue; it's a smaller copy of the main tomb and was originally decorated with blue faience tiles. Stone vessels marked with the names of earlier pharaohs were found in one part of the tomb. It seems likely that Djoser decided to relocate the tomb's contents to the new royal necropolis so that the cult of his ancestors would have been celebrated alongside his own. (It also makes Djoser's tomb a sort of king list.)

---

[i] Wilkinson, Toby A. H. *Early Dynastic Egypt.* Pg. 81.

Then, there is the Heb Sed Court for the Sed festival, complete with dummy buildings that were perhaps intended to evoke the temporary reed-mat shrines set up for the jubilee. Although the Sed festival was a thirty-year jubilee, it might originally have been intended as a kind of rejuvenation of the pharaoh rather than a simple commemoration. The coronation was reenacted on a throne platform that had two staircases (and possibly two thrones). Both crowns were used in the ceremony. There was a procession around the gods' shrines, and the pharaoh then ran a ritual race around the sides of the courtyard, which was intended to be symbolic of his bestriding the whole country.

Finally, there is the serdab chamber, which contained a near-life-sized statue of the pharaoh. This statue allowed his ka (soul or spirit) to observe the offerings made to it. A small hole allowed the ka to come and go freely.

The whole complex is Djoser's biggest claim to fame. However, he also expanded the Egyptian economy. He was the first pharaoh to begin turquoise mining in Wadi Maghareh in the Sinai Peninsula as a regular activity rather than through sporadic expeditions.

Although this book is about the pharaohs, from time to time, there are some individuals who are worth making a detour to learn about. Imhotep is one of them. He wasn't just the vizier. He was also the high priest of Ra at Heliopolis, the center of the Ra cult, and he eventually was recognized as a god, becoming the patron of medicine and healing. He carried on working for Djoser's son (or possibly brother) and successor, Djoser-tety Sekhemkhet, and is recorded in two inscriptions. One inscription is on a statue of Djoser, and the other is on Djoser-tety's pyramid. Unfortunately, only the first step of that pyramid was completed, as Djoser-tety only reigned for six or seven years.

Imhotep must have been quite a visionary. The film *The Mummy* isn't the best testament to this fascinating man.

The elite tombs around the Step Pyramid of Djoser have relief carvings and paintings that give us a picture of how the Egyptians of Djoser's day saw their world. They are shown sitting in front of tables where food has been offered for their sustenance in the afterlife. They have tightly curled wigs, ornate collars, and, in the case of Hesy-Ra, a double ink pot (for red and black ink) and a reed pen.

Unfortunately, the rest of the kings of the Third Dynasty were not as ambitious as Djoser. However, toward the end of the dynasty and the beginning of the Fourth Dynasty, two kings erected small step pyramids around Egypt. These pyramids were not intended to be tombs but rather cult objects. Huni, "the Smiter," took the Horus name Qahedjet, "his white crown is high." He appears to have built the pyramid on Elephantine island at the southern frontier, while Sneferu, the first ruler of the Fourth Dynasty, built one in the Faiyum Oasis, another frontier. Their concern must have been to make the pharaoh's power, which was very evident in Memphis, visible across the entire realm. Other small step pyramids at Edfu, Hierakonpolis, Abydos, and in the Nile Delta show how they marked their power all over Egypt.

In the earlier period, most of the king's officers had been members of the extended royal family. Over time, the concept of a meritocracy was established. Metjen worked for both Huni and Sneferu, and his tomb chapel, which can now be seen in its entirety in the Berlin Egyptian Museum, records his donations to Djoser's mother's cult and his work on irrigation and land reclamation schemes. The inscriptions also tell us that his father left him nothing except the ability to read and write. Metjen came from nothing to become one of the greatest men of the realm.

Sneferu was the pharaoh who started the Fourth Dynasty. He took the Horus name Nebmaat, meaning "lord of truth." His throne name, Sneferu, means "the one who has been made perfect."

The length of Sneferu's rule has been debated, but it likely lasted as long as forty-eight years. During this time, he built not one but three separate pyramids and continually refined the architectural concept. He started a pyramid at Meidum, about forty miles south of Saqqara. This was the first pyramid whose subsidiary buildings were planned on an axial design rather than using a rectangular enclosure. This pyramid was designed to have eight steps, making it two steps taller than Djoser's.

Eventually, Sneferu decided that simply having more steps was not enough of a change. He decided to build a completely geometrical, smooth-sided pyramid. He chose a site between Meidum and Saqqara, a place called Dahshur, and began to build what was intended to be a relatively slender structure with a fifty-four-degree slope. However, halfway through, the angle was corrected to forty-three degrees, giving the pyramid the nickname "Bent" Pyramid.

Finally, Sneferu began another pyramid, starting it off at forty-three degrees, making it the most squat-looking of all the pyramids. This was the Red Pyramid at Dahshur, which is about three-quarters of a mile away from the Bent Pyramid. The pace of building accelerated, as he also decided to convert the unfinished Meidum pyramid from a step pyramid to a true pyramid. This was not just a huge amount of construction. It also involved a huge amount of experimentation in a relatively short time. This process created knowledge that Khufu was able to use for his gigantic creation farther north on the Nile bank at Giza.

Sneferu supported his building boom through an aggressive foreign policy. He raided Libya and Nubia to capture slaves and cattle. He had a fleet of at least sixty royal boats, including his personal vessel *Praise of the Two Lands*, and imported huge amounts of cedar from Lebanon. (Egypt is very poor in timber resources.) He also created 35 royal estates and 122 cattle farms. The meat was for the royal court, not for the farmers. We know that because archaeological evidence shows that the local people at Imu, a cattle farm near the Nile Delta, had a diet that was extremely poor in meat.

Sneferu made one very important change. He was the first pharaoh to write his titles in a cartouche. This remained the standard until the end of the dynastic period.

Sneferu was succeeded by his son Khufu, also known as Cheops. Khufu took over a state that was firing on all cylinders. The irrigation system had been centralized, making the Nile Valley incredibly fertile, and new towns were being founded. State workshops were beginning to promote new styles of sculpture and even pottery across Egypt.

At the same time, religious concepts were changing. The pharaoh was still thought of as a representation of Horus, but his afterlife became entangled with the solar god Ra. The king would enjoy immortality through his ascent to the celestial realm, where he would ride in the solar barque with Ra. The great pyramids of Giza reflect the shifting conception of the afterlife as well as the increasing power of the pharaohs.

Khufu, according to Greek historians, was a tyrant. According to the Egyptians, he was a generous ruler. The Westcar Papyrus contains tales of magicians that were told at his court, but it dates from much later, during the Hyksos period, and includes tales of Djoser and Sneferu, as well as Khufu and his sons. Maybe we shouldn't rely on it any more than we rely on Shakespeare to tell the true story of Antony and Cleopatra!

Khufu is most remembered for constructing the Great Pyramid, one of the best-known monuments of ancient Egypt. It was the tallest building in the world until the Lincoln Cathedral was built in 1311. The Great Pyramid of Giza is still an amazing sight. The statistics are even more amazing. Each block of stone in the pyramid weighs five tons. Over two million blocks of stone were used. The pyramid must have taken about twenty years of work, even if we assume that a new block was placed every three minutes, night and day.[i]

The pyramid was also built with an astonishing level of precision, as it was orientated to true north to within a fragment of a degree. This required the use of advanced astronomical measurement. The shafts in the pyramid point toward the star Sirius and to two stars that rotate around the celestial north pole; the pyramid thereby unites heaven and earth in a single building.

As with Djoser's pyramid, the Great Pyramid was part of a larger complex. The pyramid itself was built on the high limestone plateau above the Nile, with a black basalt mortuary temple in front of the pyramid where the cult of the king would have been carried out after his death. A causeway led down toward the valley temple from the mortuary temple, with its dock on the river. Unfortunately, the valley temple has been lost under the modern town of Giza.

Egypt's centralized state enabled the labor force for the construction of such a magnificent monument. The forced labor system was part of Egyptian life; everyone had to work for a number of days every year for the state, though the wealthy could usually buy their way out or provide workers from their estates as substitutes. The pyramid project was a major economic focus and also delivered a political narrative.

The work teams were organized in a hierarchy. Ten teams of twenty formed a phyle, five phyles made a gang, and two gangs made a crew (two thousand workers). There were probably two crews working on the project at any one time, making four thousand workmen, but, of course, there would have been additional laborers. There would have been bakers and brewers to provide the main staples of Egyptian life. There would have been tool-makers, water carriers, staff involved in the maintenance of the workers' barracks, and kitchen staff. There would have been butchers, as the workmen had a high protein diet with lots of beef to build up their strength. There may well have been up to ten thousand people employed

---

[i] Brier, Bob. *The Murder of Tutankhamun: A True Story.* Putnam, 1998. Pg. 21.

on the plateau at some point.

Stones were split in the quarry by first making a hole using bronze chisels with a stone hammer and then filling the holes with dry wooden wedges. The wood was soaked so that it expanded and split the stone. The stones were moved on sledges or rollers, which were pulled by teams of men, and they would have been brought up the sides of the pyramid on a ramp. The blocks were moved into place first, and the outside was only carved once the stones were in place.

The tombs of the rest of the royal family, as well as the subsidiary tombs of nobles and administrators, grew up around the pyramid. These people weren't ritually killed anymore; instead, they were buried in mastabas in grid-like streets to ride on the pharaoh's coattails to the afterlife. Perniankhu, the king's dwarf, was buried nearby, and the tomb of Hetepheres, the king's mother, has been found. In her tomb was a lightweight, portable bed that she must have used on journeys.

Hemiunu, one of Khufu's nephews and the overseer of the construction projects, was also buried at Giza. His tomb contained a life-sized statue that was unusually realistic for ancient Egypt, where statues were usually quite idealized. He gives his various titles as well, which include chief justice, vizier, and "Greatest of the Five of the House of Thoth." (Thoth was the god of scribes, so this was presumably a civil service title.) The seated statue from his serdab (now in the Pelizaeus Museum in Hildesheim, Germany) is impressive. It depicts a once strong man who has become fat, complete with man boobs. However, his expression makes him look astute, forthright, and powerful.

So, what does the pyramid mean? We don't have any texts from this period that explain the concept. The late Fifth and Sixth Dynasty Pyramid Texts say that the king would rise as a star in his afterlife, which seems to match the form of the pyramid since the shafts point north. This is a definite shift from Abydos, where the tombs face east to the rising sun.

Khufu had a series of boat pits dug to contain the deconstructed planks and rigging of royal boats. One of these has been rebuilt and now resides in a museum next to the pyramid. The sun god Ra traveled through the sky on his solar barque, and the burial of the boats would have given Khufu his own boat to travel alongside the sun god.

There is one other thing that the pyramid means, and it's not theological; it's political. The pyramid was an expression of the pharaoh's absolute power.

And yet, Khufu, in contrast to his nephew and architect Hemiunu, remains unknowable. A thumb-sized ivory statuette from the temple of Khenti-Amentiu at Abydos is the only surviving portrayal of the pharaoh. Maybe Khufu was hedging his bets by sending a statuette to the lord of the west and building a boat to sail with Ra. Or maybe, as leading archaeologist Zeni Hawass thinks, the statuette is a Twenty-sixth Dynasty copy.

Khufu was succeeded by Djedefre, his son. His name means "Ra speaks," and he also added the title "son of Ra" in what must have been a slight break with the Horus tradition. He built a pyramid at Abu Rawash, located five miles north of Giza. He was succeeded by his younger brother Khafre ("Ra appears"), who returned to Giza and created his own sequence of funerary monuments—a valley temple, causeway, mortuary temple, and pyramid—next to Khufu's. Particularly interesting is the fact that Khufu's valley temple survives next to the Sphinx, which is probably also Khafre's work.

Khafre was actually quite smart when it came to designing his monument. The pyramid is not quite as tall as his father's, but it is slightly steeper. It is situated ten meters higher on the plateau, which makes it look taller.

The mortuary temple only exists in a plan, but it shows what became the standard elements of mortuary temples from that point onward. First, there was an entrance hall and a columned court with niches for statues of the pharaoh. After this, there was an inner sanctuary. The Valley Temple, where the causeway up to the pyramid starts, has a vestibule running across the front of the temple and a T-shaped pillared hall inside, where each column had a statue of Khafre standing in front of it.

Khafre was succeeded by his son Menkaure, who built the third (and smallest) of the Giza pyramids. He was given the name Netjer-er-Menkaure ("Menkaure is divine"). His main pyramid was accompanied by three smaller pyramids, which were possibly intended for Menkaure's wives.

Menkaure's valley temple survived. It was mainly built of brick, but it contained a marvelous series of nome triads (statues that show him with the goddess or god of one of the nomes (administrative districts)) on one side and the goddess Hathor on the other. They are exquisitely beautiful sculptures with a finely polished surface. They show the pharaoh striding forward confidently, slightly ahead of the goddesses. The point of the work was to show him as the pharaoh of not just Egypt as a generalized concept but also an Egypt that is regulated and organized according to Maat (order). This was perhaps a slightly bureaucratic way of thinking, but it was not out of line with the idea of the pharaoh as maintaining the divine order.

One of Menkaure's statues, with Hathor on the right and the personification of the nome of Diospolis Parva on the left. [47]

Menkaure was succeeded by his son Shepseskaf, who oddly decided to build his tomb to the south of Saqqara instead of Giza. His tomb, known as Mastabat al-Fira'un, is a two-stepped mastaba. It is not a pyramid, though it is possible that he intended to build a pyramid but simply ran out of time. He was likely the last pharaoh of the Fourth Dynasty, which is something of an anticlimax.

Userkaf founded the Fifth Dynasty. He might have been related to Khafre's family in some way, possibly through Menkaure's daughter, Khentkaus. It might be that he saw himself as reviving Egypt after an unsuccessful reign or a period of contention. It might also be possible that he felt his legitimacy needed defending. In any case, he decided to link himself with the greatness of the past by building his pyramid at the corner of Djoser's great enclosure, which was two hundred years old by that point and now represented a golden age. Userkaf might have been the first to use this trick of connecting himself with an illustrious earlier pharaoh, but he wouldn't be the last.

Userkaf took the Horus name of Iri-Maat, "the one who has accomplished order." Clearly, he felt that asserting himself as a righteous ruler was important.

Under Userkaf, the cult of Ra became predominant in Egypt. Userkaf built a temple dedicated to Ra at Abusir, which was designed as a huge mastaba with a causeway leading up to it from a valley temple. Perhaps it was intended as a mortuary temple for the setting sun so that offerings could be given to help Ra's barque sail past the dangers of the night. Userkaf also adopted the title of "Son of Ra," which became standard after his rule, confirming Djedefre's earlier rebranding of the pharaoh.

Reading between the lines, Shepseskaf might have decided that the priesthood of Ra had become too powerful and attempted to break away. In that case, Userkaf would have been returning Egypt to Maat. All of the Fifth Dynasty pharaohs that we know were in Userkaf's direct line built sun temples of their own, reaffirming the pharaoh's relationship to the god Ra.

Userkaf made an interesting innovation, as there are scenes of hunting shown in his mortuary temple. Scenes of hunting were not uncommon in Egyptian tombs, but in the case of a pharaoh's tomb, they can be read as idealizing his role in triumphing over chaos.

Userkaf was succeeded by his son Sahure, who was followed by three of his sons, the short-lived Neferefre, Shepseskare, and then Nyuserre Ini.[1] Nyuserre Ini built six pyramids at Abusir, though they were not all for himself. Two were for his queens, and others were for his mother, father (which he completed for him), and brother, who had not ruled long enough to build one. The relationship of the next three pharaohs is uncertain, though they belonged to the same family. Menkauhor Kaiu might have been Nyuserre Ini's nephew, and Djedkare Isesi could have been either a brother or a son (or even a cousin) of Menkauhor Kaiu.

The last pharaoh of the Fifth Dynasty was Unas, who was probably Djedkare's son. Like Userkaf, he built his pyramid next to Djoser's compound, but he also introduced a major innovation. Previous pyramids had burial chambers that were quite plain, but Unas decorated his burial chamber with a starry sky in the vault and the Pyramid Texts inscribed on the walls. In the antechamber, inscriptions relate to the horizon as a place of rebirth, and inscriptions in the burial chamber refer to the underworld. The 283 "utterances" are magical spells that were probably recited at the time of the king's burial and were made eternal by inscribing them in the stone.

The Pyramid Texts show that the pharaohs were quite capable of believing in two different myths since the pharaoh is identified with both Ra, the sun god who rises again every day, and with Osiris, who in Unas's day was a fairly new god. Osiris was beginning to become a more important god, though, which was perhaps why neither Djedkare nor Unas built a sun temple. Ra's importance might have been on the decline.

There is also one very odd incantation (actually two utterances, numbers 273 and 274) known as the "Cannibal Hymn." It tells how "Unas eats people and ... lives by eating gods." By eating every deity, he compels the gods' obedience. By doing so, the king would have assimilated divine powers—an almost psychopathic boast.

The kings of the Fifth Dynasty had put more and more space between them and their courtiers. Officials continued to be buried in the Giza Plateau, while the royal tombs in Saqqara and Abusir stood in glorious isolation. However, the officials' tombs of the Fifth and Sixth Dynasties are marvelous works of art and give a remarkably intimate view of

---

[1] It is important to note that king lists and archaeological evidence don't always agree. For instance, some say that Neferirkare Kakai came before Neferefre and that Neferefre is Neferirkare Kakai's son.

Egyptian life at the time. Scenes show the presentation of offerings, with lines of painted offering bearers taking food toward the false door to the burial chamber, ensuring the service of the owner in the afterlife.

Many officials told their life stories on the walls of their tombs and showed their leisure pursuits—hunting, fowling, fishing, music, board games, and feasting—and the extent of their agricultural estates. The tombs use hierarchical scaling, which is a basic form of Egyptian art. The owner of the tomb is shown in large scale, his wife and children are smaller, and his servants are miniature. (The same rule is at work in Menkaure's nome sculptures, where the gods are slightly smaller than him and also shown behind him.)

Agriculture was productive, though there was limited technology. Plows were still very basic, making a shallow furrow, and many farmers still used hoes. Wooden sickles with sharp flint teeth, which were inserted to cut the stalks of wheat, were used. Flour was milled in limestone mortars, which left the flour gritty when the soft stone broke down. This was one reason so many mummies have bad teeth.

Beekeeping was practiced in the Old Kingdom. Pottery tubes were used as hives. A sweet tooth might have been a common high-class Egyptian failing and could not have helped the dental problems caused by the gritty bread.

Some historians believe that the bureaucracy became too efficient, allowing the pharaoh to retreat into his palace and live the high life instead of actually needing to govern. For instance, one of the finest tombs at Saqqara is that of Pharaoh Nyuserre Ini's two manicurists, Khnumhotep and Niankhkhnum. (To be fair to them, they held a number of other titles, including scribe and sun priest.)

Ptahshepses, another official of Nyuserre, was his barber, manicurist, keeper of the headdress, vizier, and chief justice. However, this might reflect the fact that the pharaoh, being a god, could not be touched by those who were not ritually pure. Rather than selecting his hairdresser to become a high official, he might have selected high officials to become his personal assistants.

Whether or not Egypt had become decadent, it does appear to have run out of steam in the later Fifth Dynasty. Pyramids became smaller and were also less well built, with brick or rubble cores instead of stone. Perhaps the great period during which the Giza pyramids were built had drained the economy. After the death of Pepi II, one of the last pharaohs of the Sixth Dynasty, things started to fall apart. Pepi had ruled for sixty-four or perhaps even ninety-four years; he might have become too old to exercise power responsibly. The problem with god-kings is that no one can tell them they ought to resign.

This marked the end of the Old Kingdom and started what is known as the First Intermediate Period. Egypt was threatened by the consolidation of power in Nubia to the south, while the nomarchs, rulers of the nomes, increased their power at the expense of central authority. The Tombs of the Nobles in Aswan show how officials like Harkhuf, who brought back a pygmy for the six-year-old Pepi II, decided they would rather be buried in rock-cut tombs at home instead of in mastabas near the pharaoh.

Short-lived kings set up power in their own cities and fragmented Egypt. There were separate rulers in Memphis, Herakleopolis, and Thebes, and many of the pharaohs of the Seventh and Eighth Dynasties are known only through the king list that Seti I created at Abydos. In fact, the Seventh Dynasty appears to have been completely spurious, while most of the kings of the Eighth Dynast didn't even last a year. By the Tenth Dynasty, the pharaohs only ruled Lower Egypt, and the rest of the country was under Theban control.

And it was in Thebes that events started to take an upward turn. It is now time to fast forward to the beginning of the Middle Kingdom to witness a dramatic change in Egypt's history.

Chapter 3: Pharaohs of the Middle Kingdom

Oddly enough, the Eleventh Dynasty did not start with a pharaoh. It started with a nomarch named Intef of Thebes. Nominally, he would have served under a pharaoh; however, the breakdown of royal power and the fragmentation of Egypt meant he was able to rule Thebes relatively independently.

Intef never claimed the throne. He never took a Horus name, and he never inscribed his name in a cartouche. However, later members of the Eleventh Dynasty saw him as a founding father and always paid him respect. He managed to hold the southern provinces of Egypt together and build the foundations for a strong state. So, in a way, the Eleventh Dynasty starts with him.

His son, Mentuhotep I, is a shadowy figure. His Horus name, Tepia, "the ancestor," might have been given to him posthumously as a mark of respect. Mentuhotep's son, Sehertawy Intef I, established the family as pharaohs. Intef I laid claim to the kingship when he took his Horus name, "maker of peace in the Two Lands." Since he held only one of the two lands and was at war with Coptos, a region to the north, at the time, his Horus name was based on aspiration rather than fact. On his death, he was succeeded by his brother, who was also named Intef.

Intef II conquered the southern area down to the First Cataract at Elephantine. He might have even controlled part of Nubia. Intef II also extended his rule to the north, taking Abydos, though this still left the northern part of Egypt under the hands of the rulers of Herakleopolis, who are recognized as the Tenth Dynasty. He ruled for nearly fifty years and left the throne to his son, Intef III.

Intef III's son, Mentuhotep II, was the pharaoh who reunited Egypt. This is why the Middle Kingdom period starts halfway through the Eleventh Dynasty and not with the nomarch Intef.

In fact, the Middle Kingdom really starts partway through Mentuhotep's long reign. He had been in charge of the southern kingdom for fourteen years before an incursion from the north forced him into a war with his neighbors. The royal necropolis at Abydos had been desecrated by the Lower Egyptian army, and he could not let that go unpunished. His armies swept north, taking the northern capital, Herakleopolis (near modern-day Beni Suef). The death of Merikare, the king of Lower Egypt, left the northerners leaderless, and Mentuhotep was able to reclaim the Nile Delta. He then adopted a new Horus name, Semertawy, "the one who unites the Two Lands."

Mentuhotep made two changes that ensured the Theban dynasty's success. First, he created a strong policy of centralization, reorganizing the country and creating governors for both of the Two Lands who would keep the nomarchs under control. Secondly, he embarked on what we would now call a major PR campaign, commissioning monuments to himself throughout the country as "the living god, foremost of kings." He had himself depicted wearing the headdresses normally associated with the gods Min and Amun.

The original god of Thebes was Montu, a war god. (The name Mentuhotep, the pharaoh's birth name, means "Montu is satisfied.") However, the creator god Amun became increasingly prominent over the course of the First Intermediate Period, and Mentuhotep likely promoted the cult of Amun quite heavily. At the same time, the composite god Amun-Min evolved, uniting the creator with the god of fertility. Naturally, Thebes became the effective capital of Egypt, and the priesthood of Amun was a huge beneficiary of largess from the pharaohs of the Middle Kingdom.

Mentuhotep created a huge memorial to himself, which is one of the great monuments of the Theban necropolis. He placed his mortuary temple at Deir el-Bahri, opposite Thebes, so that it was on the route of the Procession of the Beautiful Valley. Every year, the statue of Amun was brought over the river from the temple of Karnak. In fact, Mentuhotep's temple became the procession's final destination.

The mortuary temple of Mentuhotep was both innovative and impressive, though only the foundations remain today. Most of the visitors to Hatshepsut's temple at Deir el-Bahri don't even glance at Mentuhotep's temple ruins. A garden in front of the temple was shaded by sycamore fig trees and tamarisks, and the walkway from the valley temple was guarded by seated statues of Mentuhotep. The statues on the left wore the white crown, and those on the right wore the red crown, emphasizing his reunification of the country.

The temple opened with a portico, which then opened to a courtyard, the middle of which was completely occupied by a massive building. This has been interpreted as the base of a solid pyramid, a symbol of the primeval mound or *ben-ben*, which rose above the waters and on which Amun performed the act of creation. However, this is not certain; the building might have been flat-roofed.

Behind this, a second court was dug into the cliffs. While the first part of the temple was dedicated to Montu, this part was dedicated to Amun. A hypostyle hall led to the sanctuary. The tomb itself was dug deep below the center of this temple. The reliefs here show the king not as the recipient of offerings but as the giver of offerings to the gods, which became standard iconography for future pharaohs. The pharaoh has also been cut down to size; he holds power by the grace of the gods rather than being a god.

Mentuhotep built new temples at Abydos, Aswan, Dendera, Gebelein, Elkab, and, notably, Karnak. However, his success as a ruler can be measured by the fact that apart from his mortuary temple, very few of his monuments survived. Paradoxically, his rebuilding of the Egyptian administration and economy made later rulers of Thebes wealthy enough to rebuild extensively, demolishing Mentuhotep's work to build bigger and better.

Mentuhotep III was probably quite mature when he succeeded his father, who had ruled for fifty-one years. Egypt was now at peace, so Mentuhotep III was able to look outward, sending an expedition to the Land of Punt (modern-day Ethiopia and Somalia). The three thousand men he sent under his steward Henenu's command came back with incense and perfume. They also dug wells in Wadi Hammamat, the main route to the Red Sea, to make passage easier for future expeditions.

Royal Names

Once the royal titulary had become fully established, every pharaoh took five names.

The first of these was the Horus name; this was the one used in most inscriptions, not the king's personal name. This was the name of the pharaoh as the god Horus.

The second was the Two Ladies name, which showed the pharaoh in relation to the two goddesses of Lower and Upper Egypt, Wadjet and Nekhbet, who are represented by the snake and the vulture.

The third name was the pharaoh's Golden Horus name. The exact significance of this name is still unclear.

The fourth name, the throne name, sometimes referred to as the prenomen, was announced at the coronation. Finally, the fifth name was the pharaoh's actual birth name.

A couple of examples of the full titulary include the following:

Horus, Strong Bull, whose images are born; whose laws are good, who pacifies all the gods; who brings together divine order, who pleases the gods; Re manifests himself as Lord; Living image of the Aten. (Tutankhamun)

The strong bull who appeared in Thebes and sustains the two lands; renewing births, the strong-armed one who has repelled the nine bows; who has repeated appearances, strong of troops in all lands; eternal is the truth of Ra; Seti beloved of Ptah. (Seti I)

Egyptian references were usually made to pharaohs by their Horus name, but Greek and later historians often used the king's birth name. This makes it difficult to reconcile the king lists and inscriptions with the names that Manetho gives because he wrote in Greek or with accounts of Egyptian history from outside of Egypt.

There appears to have been a crisis in the succession, as Mentuhotep IV (either the son or a brother of Mentuhotep III) is missing from several king lists. He did not reign for long, and we know about him from a few inscriptions of his reign. In his second year, he sent an expedition to Wadi Hammamat under his vizier, Amenemhat.

There is absolutely no information on what happened next. There appears to have been some conflict. The tomb of a regional governor named Khnumhotep at Beni Hasan contains scenes of Egyptians attacking Egyptians, and the governor tells a story of sailing south with Amenemhat. Possibly, Mentuhotep IV chose his vizier as the next king, or perhaps Amenemhat took power on his own account.

In any case, Amenemhat I founded the Twelfth Dynasty. He took the Horus name Sehotep ibtawy, "he who has appeased the heart of the two lands," and "the uniter" as his Golden Horus name; he might have felt he had something to prove. The *Prophecy of Neferti* might also date from his reign. The story is set in the time of Pharaoh Sneferu ("the good old days") and predicts the advent of King Ameny, who will rescue Egypt from being overrun by hostile foreigners.

Amenemhat might have had a difficult time enforcing his rule. About twenty years into his reign, he made Senwosret I (also spelled Senusret) his co-ruler, and the two kings shared rule for about a decade. Co-rulership enabled the next pharaoh to settle firmly into place before the death of the other co-ruler, easing the transition between kings. It became a common feature of future dynasties.

Co-rulership certainly worked for Amenemhat, if not quite in the way he had expected. Various sources suggest that Amenemhat was assassinated while Senwosret was absent from the capital. However, Senwosret still managed to retain power.

Halfway through his rule, Amenemhat moved the capital from Thebes to Itj-tawy ("Seizer-of-the-Two-Lands," near Cairo). He had obviously realized how being exclusively based in Thebes could be a hindrance to managing all of Egypt, as Thebes was too far to the south. Amenemhat also shored up the defenses of the country at the borders, building forts along the east side of the Nile Delta and regaining control of the fort of Buhen, which dominated the southern approach to Egypt. He appears to have been a smart ruler and set Egypt on the path to success.

Cultural Shifts

During the Middle Kingdom, there were some major shifts in religious thinking. For instance, the cult of Osiris became more widespread due to its promise of resurrection. Osiris's brother Seth (or Set) schemed against him, building a wooden chest to Osiris's exact measurements. He then offered the chest as a prize to anyone who could fit in it (similar to

Cinderella's glass slipper). As soon as Osiris got in, Seth locked up the chest and sent it sailing off to sea. The chest washed up on the shore in Lebanon, where a huge cedar tree eventually grew around it.

One day, the cedar was felled to make the central pillar of the king's palace. Isis, Osiris's wife, found out where the chest was, and she managed to recover Osiris's body and bring it back to Egypt. Seth was outraged. He cut Osiris's body into pieces and flung them around Egypt. Isis patiently gathered up the remains, all except his penis, which she could not find. After transforming herself into a kite (a bird of prey), she revived the body magically and was impregnated by it. She gave birth to the god Horus, the hawk-god.

As the king of the dead, Osiris offered hope to every Egyptian, not just the pharaoh, of an afterlife. Funerary rites that were originally exclusive to the pharaoh became democratized (at least for the upper classes). However, at the same time, a major barrier appeared: the idea of a final judgment. The heart of the deceased was thought to be weighed against a feather. Only those whose hearts weighed the same as the feather could live forever with Osiris. These pure souls were referred to as "justified" or "true of voice."

During the Middle Kingdom, the heart amulet appeared. It was intended to prevent the heart from bearing false witness when it was weighed. Scarabs also entered into common use as amulets around this time.

The Pyramid Texts, which were restricted to the pharaohs, were replaced by the Coffin Texts, which included some of the same magical spells. The corpse at this time was usually laid on its side looking east, with eyes painted on the coffin so that it could "see."

The other new arrival was the shabti, a little figure that might originally have been meant as a "replacement" mummy in case the tomb was destroyed. It was later seen as a servant for a person's ka. Shabtis were given little tools and had inscriptions telling them to present themselves for orders if the deceased was required to do any work in the afterlife.

Senwosret I built the temple of Amun-Re at Karnak, known as Ipet-Isut, "the chosen place." He sent seventeen thousand miners to Wadi Hammamat to bring back stone for the construction of the temple. The temple's north-south axis is aligned with Mentuhotep's tomb at Deir el-Bahri and clashed with the existing orientation of the town.

Just one alabaster chapel survives from Senwosret's original work, and it is exquisite. It was actually demolished and used as rubble in a later building, but the pieces were rediscovered in the 1920s and reassembled. The reliefs are of very high quality and show the pharaoh embracing the gods Amun, Horus, Min, and Ptah. A particularly interesting feature is the enumeration of all forty-two nomes of Egypt around the base of the walls. Like Menkaure's nome triads, Senwosret's chapel shows all the provinces that were subservient to the pharaoh.

Senwosret I ruled nearly half a century and set Egypt back on an upward path. He subjugated Nubia, building fortresses along the river and taking possession as far as the Second Cataract. Nubia became Egypt's main source of gold since the Eastern Desert resources were approaching exhaustion. Egypt also traded with Crete, Mesopotamia, and Syria. Thousands of Asiatic slaves arrived in Egypt as a result of these expeditions.

Senwosret was succeeded by Amenemhat II, who made several mining expeditions into Sinai and carried out a number of important building works. Amenemhat established a co-regency with Senwosret II, who developed agriculture in the Faiyum, a wetland to the west of the Nile. He created drainage canals and a dam to regulate the flow of water, reclaiming marshland and making it into farmland. Fishing in the lake became an important industry.

The town of Kahun was built around this time, and its planned layout, divided into areas for officers and for other classes, became typical of the Twelfth Dynasty. Egypt had become quite wealthy by this point; for instance, even ordinary workmen's families often had mirrors in their houses, and the streets were all drained by a central gutter. Many houses were vaulted with mudbrick arches. A papyrus with advice for gynecologists was found at Kahun and included several methods of contraception. Though not all the medicines suggested would have been effective, it is a notably pragmatic work with instructions for diagnosis that show keen observation.

Kahun was erected for the men who worked on Senwosret II's pyramid at El Lahun. The city was abandoned later, making it a particularly interesting archaeological site. Metal tools were known by this date, but stone tools were still used more often. Flint chipping was a highly skilled craft.

The inhabitants of Kahun might have worked hard, but they also knew how to play. Excavations uncovered toys, such as painted wooden dolls and whipping tops, as well as senet, a board game.

Senwosret II was succeeded by his son Senwosret III, who is seen by some Egyptologists as the greatest ruler of the Twelfth Dynasty. However, others view him as an absolute despot whose propaganda is not dissimilar from that employed by Kim Jong Un:

"How Egypt rejoices in your strong arm:

you have safeguarded its traditions."[i]

Senwosret II's statues are interesting because they often show him with protruding ears and eyes, which make him look like a weary old man. It has been suggested that the style was intended to show that he was always watching and always listening. Under Senwosret, it was not Big Brother but rather Big Pharaoh.

Senwosret III abolished the power of the nomarchs, which had been one of the reasons behind the fragmentation of the First Intermediate Period. He centralized provincial bureaucracy at his court so that the nomarchs were forced to live there, giving them no opportunity to establish a regional power base.

He continued the work of pacifying Nubia, which was again becoming rebellious, and completed the network of Nubian forts. This gave him a system of surveillance that ensured tight control of the frontier. His inscriptions show an approach to foreign expeditions that can only be described as total warfare. "I have carried off their women and brought away their dependents, burst forth to [poison] their wells, driven off their bulls, ripped up their barley, and set fire to it."[ii]

The Middle Dynasty pharaohs continued to build pyramids, though none of them approached Khufu's in size. Senwosret III built his pyramid

---

[i] Wilkinson, Toby A. H. *The Rise and Fall of Ancient Egypt: The History of a Civilization from 3000 BC to Cleopatra.* Bloomsbury Publishing, London, 2010.

[ii] Wilkinson, Toby A. H. *The Rise and Fall of Ancient Egypt: The History of a Civilization from 3000 BC to Cleopatra.*

complex at Dahshur, which included seven subsidiary pyramids for his queens, as well as a mortuary temple. The revival of pyramids might have been intended as a propaganda message linking the Twelfth Dynasty to the Old Kingdom. Senwosret III even included two Third Dynasty sarcophagi in his complex, attempting to incorporate the authority of the great Djoser into the work.

Senwosret III co-ruled for some time with his son Amenemhat III, who continued the development of the Faiyum and built two pyramids. He was the first ruler since Sneferu not to be content with just one. One pyramid was at Dahshur, the traditional royal acropolis, but the other was at Hawara in the Faiyum, showing just how important this "new" district of Egypt was to him.

Amenemhat III's rule marked a real golden age for Egypt, with wealth being funneled in from abroad and the fertility of Faiyum agriculture increasing. Amenemhat carried out an expedition to Punt, procuring incense and precious metals.

However, after the rule of these great pharaohs, Egypt fell once more on hard times. Amenemhat IV seemed to have ruled for only eight years after the death of Amenemhat III. The throne was then taken by a woman, Sobekneferu, which was unusual. Sobekneferu might have been Amenemhat IV's sister or wife.

Sobekneferu was the first woman to take the full royal titulary, with the Horus name of Meryt Re, "beloved of Re." Her birth name refers to the crocodile god Sobek, who was worshiped in the Faiyum area. She had herself depicted in male attire, though fully feminine in form.

Sobekneferu only retained power for four years. Her tomb has not yet been found. After her rule, the Twelfth Dynasty came to an end, and the Second Intermediate Period began. During this period, many kings were already aging when they took the throne, and few ruled for more than a few years. The gains that the great Twelfth Dynasty kings had made in Nubia were given up, and worse, there were new kids on the block: the Hyksos.

Hyksos is just a Greek version of the Egyptian name for foreigners, *Heka Khasut*. The Hyksos were probably Semitic tribes from the Levant. While the Hyksos, like the Nubians, became a byword for threatening foreign invaders, there is no archaeological evidence of widespread destruction. The Hyksos might have migrated into Egypt via the Nile Delta, where their capital of Avaris (Hut-Waret) was located.

Although Egypt in the Middle Kingdom had become wealthy, it had not developed the same technology as the Hyksos. The Hyksos leapfrogged Egypt, coming up with new ideas like the composite bow, the horse-drawn chariot, and body armor.

Egyptian history is rarely simple. And the history becomes really difficult to follow in the Second Intermediate Period. Again, Egypt was divided, with a line of Theban kings as well as an (unnumbered) Abydos dynasty in the south. The Fourteenth (Canaanite) Dynasty in the Nile Delta was succeeded by the Fifteenth (Hyksos) Dynasty. The Thebans became the Sixteenth Dynasty, but they were eventually conquered by the Fifteenth Dynasty. When glancing at the list of kings of Upper Egypt, it actually looks as if time ran backward.

Even though the Canaanites had Semitic names such as Yakbim and Ya'ammu, they took Egyptian throne names as Sekhaenre and Nubwoserre. Khyan, probably the fifth of the Canaanite pharaohs, adopted the royal title Ineqtaw Seuserenre Khyan, "the one who has embraced the lands, the one Ra has made strong."

Thebes continued to be ruled by Egyptians, including Intef V, Intef VI, and Intef VII; their names obviously harken back to the establishment of the Middle Kingdom by another Theban dynasty. However, it appears that these kings took their orders from the Hyksos. There is a story of Seqenenre and Apophis (Apepi) in which the Hyksos king demands Seqenenre close the hippopotamus pool in Thebes. Apophis said he could hear the noise all the way from Avaris, and it was ruining his sleep.

Finally, one of them cracked. Khaemwaset Seqenenre Tao, the eighth pharaoh of the Seventeenth Dynasty (which ruled from Thebes), marched on the Hyksos. His mummy is disfigured by massive wounds to the head, probably made by a spear and/or an ax. His body also appears to have been poorly and hurriedly mummified after decomposition had already set in.

Khaemwaset Seqenenre Tao might have been killed in battle, but his arms are completely unharmed; it appears that he did not have the chance to defend himself. It has been suggested that he was captured in a skirmish against the Hyksos and ceremonially executed on the battlefield. That would also explain the delay in starting the mummification process.

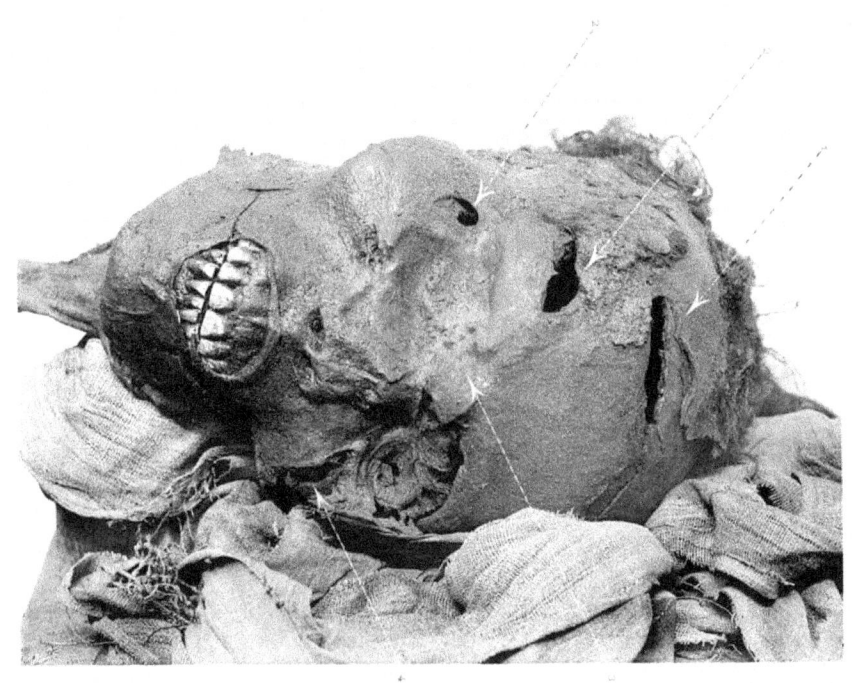

Seqenenre Tao's mummy; it is not a lovely sight. "

Kamose, Seqenenre Tao's son, continued the struggle against the Hyksos, traveling up the Nile and taking each Hyksos town or garrison in turn. He also campaigned in Nubia, and it appears that at some point in his short reign of just five years, he appointed his brother, Ahmose, as co-regent.

Kamose might have been killed in battle; he was buried in an ungilded coffin, which suggests that he never had the time to complete his tomb and order his burial equipment. His brother, Ahmose I, had better luck. He drove the Hyksos out of Egypt and began the Eighteenth Dynasty and the New Kingdom. He pushed northward along the Nile, but instead of heading for the Hyksos capital of Avaris, he bypassed it to take the border town of Tjaru. This cut the Hyksos off from any possible aid from the Canaanites. The campaign was recorded by Ahmose, son of Ebana, who wrote it on the walls of his tomb in El Kab.

Ahmose married several of his sisters, with Ahmose-Nefertari as his chief wife. He also built the last extant royal pyramid at Abydos. It must have been a remarkably steep pyramid judging from the remaining two courses of casing stones; unfortunately, the pyramid collapsed before modern times, so it is now just a low heap. His cult continued at Abydos, at least until the time of Ramesses II; that alone shows that Ahmose was considered one of the greatest kings of Egypt. This pyramid was the last ever built as part of a mortuary complex in Egypt, and it marks the end of an era—and the beginning of a new one.

Chapter 4: Hatshepsut and Akhenaten

Ahmose I was the first pharaoh of the New Kingdom. Apart from the pyramids, the best-known Egyptian monuments and artifacts—Tutankhamun's funerary mask, the temple of Karnak, and the tombs of the Valley of the Kings—date from this period, which saw the height of Egyptian power and wealth.

The New Kingdom saw the creation of imperial aspirations. Extending the frontiers of Egypt was a new desire. The Egyptians wanted more than just to trade with other countries; they also wanted to formally add them to the Egyptian kingdom.

The New Kingdom saw much greater restrictions placed on royal women. Sibling marriage was already practiced, keeping the pharaoh's sisters in the family, but royal women were no longer allowed to marry outside the family at all. The king's son was also his son-in-law. There was no possibility of an official married to a princess trying to take power in his wife's name.

Yet, paradoxically, some of the most powerful women in Egypt's history lived during the New Kingdom. The first of these was Ahhotep, Ahmose I's mother; she had held the reins of power, which she possibly shared with her mother, Tetisheri, during her son's childhood. She remained influential during his adult life as well. Ahhotep was buried with a necklace of flies, which was the supreme award for bravery in battle, and a stela describes her as the ruler of Egypt who had united the people, a phrase usually used to describe the pharaoh.

Ahmose married his sister Ahmose-Nefertari, who inherited the same titles as Ahhotep (King's Daughter, King's Sister, and King's Great Wife). However, she was also given the title God's Wife of Amun, making her effectively the joint head of Karnak and creating strong links between the state god and the king's family. This office gave royal wives a platform for power, particularly during regencies. Ahmose-Nefertari was likely the power behind the throne during the early reign of Amenhotep I.

Amenhotep I made a major change in funerary architecture. Ever since the Old Kingdom, the king's tomb had been associated with a mastaba, pyramid, or mortuary temple. However, grave robbers had become a menace. Amenhotep decided to combat the bandits by placing the tomb and mortuary temple in different locations and then keeping the site of the tomb secret. In fact, he hid his tomb so well that it has yet to be found.

For the site of the tomb to remain secret, a different approach was needed. The forced labor system of the Old Kingdom would not work. Under Amenhotep or perhaps his successor, Thutmose I, a tomb workers' village was founded called Set-Maat, "the place of truth"; its modern name is Deir el-Medina. Specialized workers, including stone carvers and painters, lived in the village behind mudbrick walls and were provided with the goods they needed by the state in return for their work. Unlike most workers, they did not have the time (or the soil since the village was in a rocky valley) to grow their own food. Amenhotep I was later worshiped as a god at Deir el-Medina, suggesting that he was the founding patron of the village.

Though most of Amenhotep I's monuments were replaced by later buildings, none of the Valley of the Kings and none of the buildings at Karnak would look the way they do today without his input. He built a huge pylon doorway at Karnak, marked "horizon," to make the temple into a microcosm, the place where the sun rose and set. He also created a new alabaster barque shrine. He saw his Egypt as a return to the "good old days" of the Twelfth Dynasty, which had ended almost three centuries before his reign began.

Amenhotep appears to have had no sons, as he associated the already middle-aged Thutmose with him during his rule (their names appear together on the alabaster barque that Amenhotep gave to the temple of Karnak). This was an imaginative way to reuse the co-rulership that Amenemhat had given Senwosret to address the main problem of an inherited kingship: the potential lack of a legitimate successor. Amenhotep probably already knew Thutmose well from working with him. He made a good choice.

Thutmose I expanded the Egyptian empire, defeating the Kingdom of Kush to expand in Nubia. He dragged his ships around the dangerous Third Cataract rapids and took Kerma, the Kushite capital. He then took the desert route to just beyond the Fourth Cataract, where he carved a huge inscription into the quartz rock at Hagar el-Merwa. His daughter, Hatshepsut, was with him when he took Egypt's armies farther south than they had ever been before. Her name is included in the inscription.

Thutmose then forced his way into Mesopotamia to the east, where the Mitanni Kingdom was becoming more powerful. Naturally, he carved a massive stela beside the Euphrates to record his campaign. He campaigned in Syria and Lebanon as well. Tribute from his conquests created wealth and led to massive economic expansion. There was an increased flow of materials from the east and south, including cedar from Lebanon for building and gold, slaves, cattle, ivory, and ebony from Nubia. During Thutmose's time, metal tools became more widespread than stone tools in towns and workmen's villages. Egypt had finally made a great technological leap forward.

Thutmose I was the first pharaoh to build a tomb in the Valley of the Kings (as far as we know). Ineni, his overseer of projects, emphasized the secrecy of the site:

"I inspected the excavation of the cliff-tomb of his majesty, alone, no one seeing, no one hearing ... It was a work of my heart, my virtue was wisdom; there was not given to me a command by an elder. I shall be praised because of my wisdom after years, by those who shall imitate that which I have done."[i]

Thutmose's reign lasted just over a decade, but what a decade it was! However, his succession plans unraveled. His two older sons, Wadjmose and Amenmose, had been promoted to positions usually given to an intended successor, such as Great General of the Army, but both died. They probably died in their twenties. This left only the young Thutmose II, who was possibly not in the best of health. He was married to Hatshepsut, Thutmose I's eldest daughter, which made her his half-sister. (Hatshepsut's mother was Ahmose, Thutmose I's Great Royal Wife, while Thutmose II was born to a minor wife, Mutnofret.) They had a daughter,

---

[i] Brier, Bob. *The Murder of Tutankhamun: A True Story.* Pg. 34.

Neferure, but Thutmose appears to have died after reigning only three years (some scholars believe he ruled for thirteen or possibly even eighteen years). His heir, Thutmose III, was Hatshepsut's stepson, and he was probably only two years old when he became pharaoh.

Hatshepsut became the regent for her stepson, just as her mother, Ahmose, had done during Thutmose II's reign. The two women were undeniably powerful. However, Hatshepsut was different. She took the name and attributes of a pharaoh and ruled on her own account. She had herself crowned and acknowledged her mother Ahmose as the King's Mother. She was King Hatshepsut; there was no Egyptian word for "queen," and what we would now call a queen had the title of King's Wife or King's Mother.

Gradually, Hatshepsut developed her image. At first, she was portrayed as a woman wearing the atef crown (ram's horns and tall feathers), but later, she had herself portrayed as fully male, wearing the pharaoh's kilt and a false beard. Gradually she took on more and more masculine attributes. The earliest Osiris statues in her funerary temple had yellow skin (conventionally female), but the later ones took on the full red ochre of masculinity.

Hatshepsut took advantage of every possibility she could to shore up her place as pharaoh. For instance, although she portrayed herself as the successor to Thutmose I, she also created the story of her divine birth. She depicts the King's Mother, Ahmose, receiving the ankh of life from Amun, who is disguised as the queen's husband. As the child of Amun, Hatshepsut could legitimize her rule. She was Useret-kau Wadjyt-renput Nejteret-kau Maatkare Khenemetamun Hatshepsut, "mighty of Ka, flourishing of years, divine of appearance, the soul of Re is truth, united with Amun, foremost of noble ladies."

She was a worthy successor to her father, Thutmose I, though she took up trade rather than warfare. She sponsored a major expedition to Punt; incense trees and other rarities were brought back to her court. Previous expeditions to Punt had been made by successful kings, such as Pepi I, Mentuhotep II, Amenemhat I, and Senwosret I, so by making such an expedition, she asserted her rightful place in the line of succession.

Hatshepsut brought in her own coterie of officials, which included Hapuseneb as the first prophet of Amun. Hapuseneb took over every title associated with the temple. He was also the overseer of other temples and centralized the Egyptian religious establishment in a new way. Ahmose

Pen Nekhbet became Hatshepsut's treasurer; he was a nobleman and a former military commander. She appointed Useramen as her vizier in the south.

The most famous of her officials, though, was Senenmut. He was the architect of Hatshepsut's funerary complex, as well as her vizier. Senenmut was of low birth, but it's evident that by this time, bureaucracy could be used as a way to enrich a person's lifestyle. He was a man from nowhere, which meant he had no other loyalties.

Senenmut was also an innovator. For instance, as the tutor to Hatshepsut's daughter Neferure, he had himself portrayed holding the royal child or holding a cryptogram of Hatshepsut's name. He was the first non-pharaoh to separate his tomb chapel from his tomb, although others soon copied him. He also designed the amazing mortuary temple at Deir el-Bahri for Hatshepsut, with its rising ramps and colonnaded porticoes under a half-moon of the cliff face. Incense trees from Punt were planted in the gardens in front of the temple, and unusually, the carved reliefs celebrate not a war campaign but the famous expedition to Punt.

Hatshepsut's mortuary temple at Deir el-Bahri.[49]

Hatshepsut continued to build at Karnak. She created the massive eighth pylon, the first monumental sandstone structure, and the Red Chapel, which was made of deep red quartzite. She also ordered the two great obelisks for Karnak.

The Karnak temple was of great importance to her; she had been the God's Wife of Amun before passing the title to her daughter Neferure. She also claimed that Amun had marked her for rulership in a vision. The barque of the god, containing his image, refused to perform its regular circuit of the temple and forced the priests to take it to Hatshepsut. In the chapel of Maat, Amun invested her as God's Wife.

Was this just propaganda, or did Hatshepsut believe it? We will never know. But what's interesting is that her stepson, Thutmose III, claimed divine inspiration in an inscription at Karnak. The barque of Amun circled a hall of the temple where the young sons of Thutmose II had been brought to choose a successor. The barque bowed before the infant prince.

Hatshepsut reigned for twenty-two years, and she disappeared from history in 1458 BCE. Perhaps opposition to a female ruler allowed Thutmose III to claim sole rule. An unusual inscription on her funerary temple states, "He who shall do her homage shall live, he who shall speak evil in blasphemy of her Majesty shall die." This may be a sign of conflicts later in her reign. Or perhaps she simply died. She can hardly have been much older than fifty, and it is possible she was even younger.

Although Thutmose III appears to have paid Hatshepsut due respect at the beginning of his reign, he later decided to erase her inscriptions and her image. He completed her Red Chapel, but five years later, he made the decision to destroy it. Twenty-five years after her death, he decided to destroy all traces of her as king. However, images of her as the Great Royal Wife were untouched.

Thutmose III expanded Egypt to its greatest extent during his fifty-four-year reign. He was a sportsman, soldier, athlete, and strongman. He shot an arrow right through a copper target and hunted elephants like his grandfather, Thutmose I. Thutmose III also portrayed himself as a military genius. In fourteen separate campaigns to the north, he defeated the growing power of Mitanni and then marched east. He set up a stela next to his grandfather's inscription on the Euphrates. Thutmose III was something of a risk-taker. When his commanders advised him to take one of the two "safer" routes to Megiddo, he insisted on taking the more direct but dangerous, narrow pass through the mountains, enabling him to surprise the Canaanite forces and defeat them.

He brought back Syrian wives and also founded a harem at Medinet el-Gurob. It was not just a place for the women of the royal family; it was also a major center for textile production. Thutmose III created a king list in his Festival Hall at Karnak. It shows only sixty-one rulers from Sneferu to Thutmose III, leaving out the first three dynasties, most of the Thirteenth Dynasty, and Hatshepsut. We have to remember that the king lists are not so much a historical document as a political and ideological document that was meant to legitimize the ruler by placing him in an unbroken legitimate line. In this case, the king list was meant to elbow out the woman who had been his co-ruler.

Perhaps the decision to erase Hatshepsut's memory was motivated by the death of his eldest son, the crown prince Amenemhat. Instead, the much younger Amenhotep II was announced as co-ruler with Thutmose and became his eventual successor. He was another warlike pharaoh whose eastern campaigns brought tremendous wealth to Egypt.

His successor, Thutmose IV (you may have noticed the lack of imagination in naming conventions in the Eighteenth Dynasty), has a unique claim. When he was out hunting in Giza, the god Horemakhet, "Horus of the Horizon," spoke to him, promising him the kingship if he rescued the Sphinx from the sand that covered it. It is possible that he usurped the throne from his older brothers.

Amenhotep III, Thutmose IV's son, promoted building projects, creating much of the Luxor Temple. Though he was the legitimate heir, he adopted Hatshepsut's idea of divine conception in reliefs, which show how he was conceived by Amun. Amenhotep is sometimes called the "sun king," much like the glorious monarch Louis XIV of France. He was also a worshiper of Amun-Re (or Amun-Ra). Amenhotep III took the title "Dazzling Sun Disk of All the Land."

Amenhotep III continued the New Kingdom's expansionist trend, though he made Egypt great through diplomacy rather than warfare. His only military action was a small-scale punitive skirmish in Nubia. He married the sister of King Tushratta of Mitanni and took another wife from Babylon, though his Great Royal Wife was the daughter of a commoner. Her name was Tiy or Tiye. He also married two of his own daughters, Sitamun and Iset, but his request to "send very beautiful women, but none with shrill voices" indicates that he ended up feeling hen-pecked.[1]

---

[1] Redford, Donald B. *Akhenaten: The Heretic King*. Princeton University Press, Princeton, 1984. Pg. 37.

His reign saw a great boom in construction. He built temples at Heliopolis, Elephantine, El Kab, Memphis, and Thebes. As mentioned, he created a new temple at Luxor, which had originally just been the shrine marking the end of the Pet festival, during which two barques carried the images of Amun and Mut on their honeymoon to the "harem of the south." Unusually, the Luxor Temple had an open courtyard, reflecting Amenhotep III's use of solar theology. He also created an avenue of sphinxes connecting the temples of Karnak and Luxor. At the Opet festival, the pharaoh communed with the god Amun-Re when his barque was taken into the temple; he emerged from the privacy of the shrine rejuvenated by Amun-Re's ka.

Amenhotep built the palace of Malkata opposite the Luxor Temple. Queen Tiye had a lake made, where she could sail her barge "Aten is Shining." Though the god Aten, the sun disk, had been worshiped since the Twelfth Dynasty, this was his breakthrough to the big time. Amenhotep built temple-towns throughout Nubia as trade centers, integrating Nubia into Egyptian religion and society.

Amenhotep was a master of propaganda, and he pushed out commemorative scarabs carved with the major events of his reign. There is an inscription that reads, "Tally of the lions which His Majesty has bagged through personal archery from Year 1 to Year 10: 102 fierce lions."[i]

However, his mummy tells a different story. By the time Amenhotep III died, he was fat and bald. He had bad teeth and painful abscesses in his mouth. When he died around 1352 BCE, he was mummified using a new technique. The embalmers injected resins under the skin to give his mummy a more lifelike appearance.

Amenhotep III was succeeded not by his oldest son, who died young, but by the very well-known Amenhotep IV.

If you haven't heard of Amenhotep IV, that may be because he changed his birth name to Akhenaten, "effective for the Aten" or "living spirit of the Aten." He also changed all his other regal names except his throne name, Nefer-kheperu-Re.)

Akhenaten might have suppressed many of the records of the earlier part of his reign, as there is a strange hiatus between his father's death and his first records as Akhenaten. He sponsored the worship of Aten, which

---

[i] Redford, Donald B. *Akhenaten: The Heretic King*. Pg. 38.

had been dear to his father and mother, but he also sought to suppress all other gods. This created a form of monotheism, something that was completely alien to Egyptian thought. Until Akhenaten's time, syncretism had allowed a newly popular god to meld himself into one or more of the older gods, as Amun had done with Min and Re. Akhenaten excluded all other deities from the worship of Aten.

Akhenaten also moved the capital from Thebes, the City of Amun, to the new city of Akhetaten (today's Tell el-Amarna). The boundary stelae of Akhetaten mark out a huge area. All of them were carved with vignettes of the royal family worshiping the sun god. All the courts of Akhenaten's sun temples were open to the sky. At Amarna, there are 365 offering tables on each side of the main temple. Akhenaten also built temples to the sun disk at Heliopolis and Memphis, as well as in Nubia. At Karnak, he had inscriptions re-cut to show his new name. He appointed new officers to his cabinet, including Ay, who was possibly related to Akhenaten's mother, Tiye, and he seems to have always been accompanied by troops. Perhaps his rule was not secure.

All Egyptian art is religious art, so the huge religious changes brought about by Akhenaten required a change in artistic style. The regular canon of proportions was abolished, and the royal family was depicted with elongated faces, huge buttocks, and stick-thin arms and legs. Intimate scenes of the royal family were created for the first time rather than only scenes of offerings or warfare. While some reliefs maintain the regular hierarchical proportions of the larger pharaoh, smaller queen, and much smaller princesses, others show Akhenaten and Nefertiti as the same size, which was revolutionary. In a way, the royal family became the representatives of the Egyptian people, and Akhenaten became the sole intercessor, making the royal family the only way in which ordinary mortals could gain Aten's blessing.

A new iconography: Akhenaten and his family worshiping the Aten sun disk.⁵⁰

Aten is shown only as a sun disk, with the rays reaching out to the royal family. There is no human figure of the god; he is a pure abstraction. There is a positive refusal of mythology in the way he is shown. Even tiny details are changed; on sistrums, jingling percussion instruments used by Egyptian women, the head of the cow-goddess Hathor, which had always decorated them, was replaced by a flower.

Akhenaten remains a puzzle. Some see him as the first monotheist, a visionary prophet, together with his wife, Nefertiti. American Egyptologist Bob Brier thinks of him as a Californian drop-out; Canadian Egyptologist Donald Redford thinks he was stupid, petty, and egotistical. English historian Cyril Aldred believes he was an enlightened ruler whose ideals were betrayed by smaller men. Historical records show that Akhenaten delegated the government to a far greater extent than earlier pharaohs and neglected foreign policy, but was this because he was living in a dream or in religious ecstasy or because he believed the civil service should do its job. Of course, it's possible that he simply didn't care enough. Akhenaten seems tantalizingly close in the reliefs of his family, but ultimately, the man behind the image of the pharaoh remains unknowable. His motto, "Living in Truth," is poignant, but what truth he lived by, we do not really know.

Even the Amarna style puzzles Egyptologists. British Egyptologist Dominic Montserrat compares the Amarna style to socialist realism, a totalitarian and idealized representation of the world. Brier believes that the pharaoh had Marfan syndrome, which affects the body's connective tissue and makes the limbs elongated and the joints weak and loose. Perhaps the treatment of the pharaoh might have been intended to show him not in a "human" body but in a divine one.

In the later years of his reign, Akhenaten saw plague ravage the land. Four of his children died. His mother, Tiye, died in the same year as his daughter, Meketaten. In 1336 BCE (or maybe 1334; exact dates are hard to find when looking so far in the past), Akhenaten went to meet Aten after ruling for seventeen years.

What happened after that is hard to work out. There appears to have been a pharaoh named Smenkhkare, who had possibly been a co-ruler with Akhenaten. He married Akhenaten's daughter, Meritaten. He might have been Akhenaten's brother or son. He was succeeded (or possibly preceded) by a female pharaoh named Neferneferuaten, who might have been Nefertiti or Meritaten. To make matters even less clear, Smenkhkare and Neferneferuaten shared the same throne name, Ankhkheperure. Neither of these pharaohs ruled very long. Smenkhkare has been identified with the male mummy found in a woman's coffin in Tomb KV55, but it is not certain if the body is his. The KV55 mummy has also been identified as Akhenaten, who was reburied after the abandonment of Amarna. (As you can tell, this period of Egyptian history is full of uncertainty.)

The next pharaoh took the throne name Nebkheperure, "lord of the forms of Re." He married the third daughter of Akhenaten, Ankhesenamun, who had already been married to two pharaohs, her father Akhenaten and her possible half-brother Smenkhkare. Three years later, Nebkheperure moved the capital from Akhetaten back to Thebes, and the worship of the old gods resumed. Akhenaten's Amarna experiment had failed.

You probably haven't heard of Nebkheperure. He came to the throne as a child, around the age of eight or nine, and only reigned for nine or ten years. He was a relatively unimportant pharaoh.

However, he is one of the most famous pharaohs due to the almost immaculate preservation of his tomb. While you may not know him by his throne name, you more than likely know him by his birth name, Tutankhaten, or, as he was later renamed, Tutankhamun.

Chapter 5: The Boy King: Tutankhamun's Reign and His Tomb

Tutankhamun owes his fame to an accident and the fact that Ramesses VI decided to create a tomb higher up the side of the Valley of the Kings. The debris from the excavations simply slid down the slope, covering the access to Tutankhamun's tomb with a thick layer of limestone rubble and protecting it from tomb robbers. So, when Howard Carter discovered the tomb in 1922 (tipped off by a young Egyptian, Hussein Abd el-Rassul), it was virtually intact.

But without the discovery of the wonderful things Carter saw inside the tomb, Tutankhamun would have been a relatively insignificant king. In fact, we might have never known about him at all. His name, like Akhenaten and Hatshepsut, was omitted from the king lists that were drawn up by Seti I and Ramesses II. In 1905, James Henry Breasted published his extensive history of Egypt based on inscriptions that he had copied for over eleven years; Tutankhamun got less than a page.

Tutankhamun was only eight or nine when he succeeded to the throne. It's likely that the real power behind the throne was Ay, a high official under Akhenaten. He was probably the great-uncle of Tutankhamun, Tiye's brother, although it has sometimes been speculated that he was the father of Nefertiti (his wife was either her mother or her wet nurse).

Tutankhamun's reign picked up where Amenhotep III left off. Akhenaten's innovations were undone, one by one. The Great Temple of the Aten at Karnak was dismantled, and the talatat (very small building blocks, which were unusual in Egypt and distinguished the work of Akhenaten's reign) were reused in other constructions. The capital was moved back to Thebes, and the cult of Amun was reestablished. A new building campaign began at Luxor, where Tutankhamun had Amenhotep III's work completed. He also finished the Avenue of Sphinxes. One solitary sphinx has Tutankhamun's face.

Tutankhamun erected a stela, known as the Restoration Stela, at Karnak. It claimed that "He restored everything that was ruined, to be his monument forever and ever. He ... has restored Maat to her place."[i] All of Egypt's troubles were blamed on the closure of the temples. Since the temples were economic centers that owned farms and production facilities, this was quite likely true and not just a theological assertion. Temple incomes were restored and even increased under Tutankhamun.

The procession from Karnak to Luxor during the Opet festival was reinstated, which must have been a popular decision with the local population since the festival included eleven days of feasting paid for by the pharaoh.

It must have been somewhat confusing for the young pharaoh, though. He had never known any cult other than Aten, so all these gods and rites would have been quite new to him.

Despite the changes, there was an impressive continuity of personnel in the new regime. Ay had already built himself a fine tomb in Amarna, showing his high status as an official under Akhenaten, but he relinquished it and built another in the western Valley of the Kings. Horemheb, Akhenaten's general, continued to serve under the next four pharaohs. Maya, who became overseer of the treasury under Tutankhamun, might have worked under Amenhotep III and kept his post for the next two pharaohs after Tutankhamun.[ii]

Tomb KV62, Tutankhamun's tomb, was probably not originally a royal tomb. The tomb is less extensively decorated than other royal tombs of

---

[i] Booth, Charlotte. *The Boy Behind the Mask: Meeting the Real Tutankhamun*. Oneworld, Oxford, 2007.

[ii] By the way, Maya's tomb in Saqqara is interesting for the light its inscriptions cast on ancient Egyptian tourism. It mentions "those who want to divert themselves in the west"—tourists who wanted to visit Giza and Saqqara to see the ancient monuments.

the time, so it might have originally been intended for Ay or another high official. Tutankhamun had already commanded a larger tomb be made ready for him—most pharaohs started work on their tombs and mortuary temples as soon as they put on the double crown—but it might not have been finished, or it might have been commandeered by one of his successors.

The best things are said to come in small packages, though. When Carter discovered the tomb, he found it crammed full of incredible artifacts, ranging from golden statuettes to model boats, portable beds, and dismantled chariots. There were also 413 shabtis and 26 wine jars. (That's only just over half the amount of wine that was buried with "Scorpion" in Tomb U-j at Abydos. Maybe King Tut wasn't a big drinker.)

The tomb was crammed with items, which may reflect the fact that the pharaoh's entire panoply of funerary equipment was forced into a much smaller tomb than usual. If the tombs of other pharaohs of the New Kingdom had come down to us intact, we likely would have seen similar contents but arranged in a more orderly way. It took Carter ten years to catalog the tomb's contents; there were 5,398 items.

There were other oddities about Tutankhamun's burial. Tutankhamun appeared to have been buried after the usual seventy days after death. He was buried nine or ten months later, according to Toby Wilkinson. And the embalmers did a shoddy job. They managed to smash up some of his skull and poured on so much resin that the mummy was effectively stuck in its coffin with black toffee. (However, the better preservation of other mummies from the New Kingdom in the Deir el-Bahri cache might be due to the fact that they were taken out of their coffins relatively early on before the resins became too hard.)

Some of the artifacts in the tomb were originally made for his predecessors, Akhenaten and Neferneferuaten. Some of these items bear those pharaohs' names, while others were re-inscribed. Maybe there was a bit of a hurry to get the tomb furnished. Less than half of the food boxes actually contain what's written on the label, so something had clearly gone wrong.

All of these oddities suggest that Tutankhamun's death was unexpected. Some Egyptologists believe he was murdered or that he died a few months after a riding accident injured his leg. However, the plague had taken many of the royal family living in Amarna. Tutankhamun wasn't the healthiest individual; he had a club foot, an overbite, and a slight cleft palate. He also had suffered repeated malarial episodes. Maybe it was the malaria that did him in. Despite various analyses of the mummy, the cause of his death is still uncertain. We only know that he was about nineteen years old when he died.

Tutankhamun was not the only inhabitant of his tomb. Two mummified fetuses were buried with him; it is possible they were his stillborn daughters. As they never lived to draw breath, they were not named. They are simply labeled "Osiris," the reborn god.

Other members of his family were also present in spirit. A series of tiny coffins contained a lock of his grandmother Tiy's hair, and there were mementos of Amenhotep III as well. Were these accidental inclusions, or did Tutankhamun treasure these souvenirs of his ancestors?

Ankhesenamun, Tutankhamun's wife (and possibly his sister), is also present in the tomb, as she is portrayed with her husband on numerous artifacts. The two are shown together in intimate scenes that are highly reminiscent of the Amarna style. She gives Tutankhamun flowers, hands him an arrow to shoot with, offers him a lotus, holds his arm, and leans forward to touch his shoulder.

It's tempting to read this as the story of a youthful, loving marriage. Carter certainly did, seeing the floral garland laid on top of the outer coffin as having been left by a grieving young widow. However, the fact is that by that time, Ankhesenamun had already been married to her father and had probably had two miscarriages (if she was the mother of the two fetuses in her husband's tomb). The apparent intimacy of these scenes may be just as misleading as the messages of power and majesty contained in the usual pharaonic images of smiting enemies or making offerings to the gods.

Tutankhamun's tomb tells us a great deal more about daily life in the New Kingdom than it does about the teenager who was buried in it due to the wide-ranging nature of the artifacts contained in it. For instance, the tomb contained composite bows, which were more powerful than earlier single-piece bows. They demonstrate a fairly recent technological transfer from the Middle East, as do the chariots that Egypt had taken from the Hyksos. The tomb contained light furniture made for a peripatetic court and chests for the pharaoh's linen. Yes, that is right; we even know what Tutankhamun's underwear looked like.

(Toby Wilkinson's book *Tutankhamun's Trumpets* uses the artifacts in Tutankhamun's tomb to tell the story of Egyptian history. It's a great compressed read if you're heading to Egypt for the first time and want to understand the culture of ancient Egypt.)

As with Akhenaten, it's difficult to tell exactly what happened after Tutankhamun died. The evidence is fragmentary and can be interpreted in different ways. Two things are certain, though.

The first is that a Great Royal Wife sent a letter to Suppiluliumas the Hittite after her husband's death, asking for him to give her one of his sons as a husband. After checking the situation out, he sent his son Zidanza. However, Zidanza was murdered as soon as he entered Egypt. The letter survived in the Hittite archives at Hattusa; however, the Great Royal Wife is not identified.

The second is that Ay, Tutankhamun's vizier, succeeded him as pharaoh, although he was not of royal blood. Ay is shown in the tomb as the leopard-skin-wearing *sem* priest. He performed the important "opening of the mouth" ritual at Tutankhamun's funeral; this rite was almost always performed by the pharaoh's eldest son and successor. By taking on that role, Ay effectively took power. He then married Ankhesenamun, who might have been his granddaughter, though his first wife, Tey, became the Great Royal Wife. Only Tey is shown in his tomb.

American Egyptologist Bob Brier is certain that Tutankhamun was murdered, and he makes a good case that Ay was the murderer and that he did away with Ankhesenamun as soon as the transfer of power was secure. However, other interpretations are possible. Perhaps Ankhesenamun was striking out in the direction Hatshepsut had taken, aiming to rule in her own right. Perhaps Ay was pushed into the job by the other officials of the royal household. Perhaps they wanted to ensure Egypt never went back to the Aten heresy or fell into chaos again.

Ay only reigned for three years. He did manage to get a nicer tomb than his predecessor; in fact, it's been suggested that Tutankhamun was buried in the tomb Ay had started building for himself and that Ay took over the tomb Tutankhamun had begun at WV23.

Ay apparently designated his son, Nakhtmin, as his successor. However, upon Ay's death, General Horemheb became pharaoh. Nakhtmin disappeared without a trace.

Horemheb is probably the most interesting of the three pharaohs mentioned in this chapter. Unlike Ay, who was not of royal blood but was at least a member of the nobility, Horemheb was a commoner. He had risen from nothing, much like Hatshepsut's steward Senenmut. Tutankhamun had actually made Horemheb his heir, though Ay had somehow managed to take over. (Horemheb might have been off on a military campaign at the time.)

Horemheb dated his rule from the end of Amenhotep III's reign, wiping out the previous four kings and thirty years in a single stroke of the chisel. He purged the bureaucracy and set up a stela at Karnak to record his reforms. He also reformed the army and restored the priesthood of Amun at Karnak. Horemheb appointed many of his own officers as priests to retain control of the institution.

During the Amarna period, Egypt had lost territory. Horemheb regained much of it. He put Egypt back on an even keel after the chaotic Amarna period and its aftermath. And he did one more thing, which was of huge importance for the path Egypt was to take in the future. Although Horemheb lacked sons, he appointed a mature successor who was not only his vizier and an experienced army commander but also had a son and grandson as potential heirs. This man was Piramesses or Paramessu. He became Pharaoh Ramesses I and started a new dynasty.

Chapter 6: Ramesses II the Great: A Pharaoh's Legacy

Ramesses I saw himself as returning Egypt to its past greatness, so he selected his royal names to suit that. His title echoes that of Ahmose I, founder of the Eighteenth Dynasty and the New Kingdom and the conqueror of the Hyksos. Perhaps as a northerner (only a northerner would call his son "Seti" after the god Seth), he felt he needed a little extra legitimacy. His full names were Ka nakht wadj nesyt, Kha em nisut mi Itemu, Semenmaat khet tawy, Menpehtyra, Ra-messu: "Horus the strong bull, flourishing in kingship, ascending as king like Atum, restoring Maat throughout the two lands, established by the strength of Re, Re has birthed him."

Ramesses might have been, to some extent, a placeholder, as he was already quite old when he was made Horemheb's heir. Ramesses's son, Seti, would obviously inherit the throne within a few years. Seti was already a promising young man; he acted as vizier under Horemheb, as well as under his father. Ramesses I quickly made him his co-ruler. Seti set out in short order to raid Canaanite territory, winning relatively little terrain but sending a warning to the Levantine kingdoms that the Egyptian empire was back.

Ramesses began the hypostyle hall at Karnak, but he died in the second year of his reign. Like Tutankhamun, he ended up buried in haste in an unfinished tomb (KV16), which had a single room. There had not even been time to carve his sarcophagus, so it had to be painted with the ritual inscriptions. They were evidently painted too quickly, as they contained a number of errors. His mummy got around, making him (posthumously) the most well traveled of all the pharaohs. It was first relocated to the Deir el-Bahri cache, and then it was stolen and sold to the US. After many years in the Niagara Falls Museum and then Atlanta, he was finally repatriated in 2003. He now rests at the Luxor Museum.

This chapter is about Ramesses the Great, Ramesses II, but Seti I arguably also deserves the title of "Great." His throne titles were more aggressive than his father's, stressing not just a renaissance but also a return to expanding the empire: "The strong bull who appears in Thebes and sustained the two lands; renewing births [i.e., a renaissance], the strong-armed one who has repelled the nine bows [enemies of Egypt]; he who renews the crowns, who subjugates the nine bows in all lands; established is the truth of Ra; Seti beloved of Ptah."

His throne name, Menmaatre, borrows from the two greatest kings of the previous dynasty: Thutmose III (Menkheperre, "established is the manifestation of Ra") and the "sun king," Amenhotep III (Nebmaatre, "Ra is lord of truth"). Unlike earlier pharaohs, Seti wasn't looking back to the golden age of the Old Kingdom; his aims were limited to regaining the wealth and status of Egypt before the heretic Akhenaten.

Before he became a pharaoh-in-waiting, Seti married the daughter of an army officer, Tuya. His son, Ramesses, appears to have done so as well, as his wife, Nefertari, never used the title King's Daughter, though she was probably from one of the elite families. Interestingly, though Seti wanted to restore pre-Amarna art conventions, he was quite innovative in his own portrayals. He decided to show himself sporting a braided hairstyle that was popular in the army.

Seti I, with his hooked nose and bright red hair, must have been a striking man. His mummy has a calm dignity that is unforgettable. He was a hard worker, engaging in major military actions and starting a large program of construction works. He kept the old vizier, Nebamun, who had been in place since Horemheb's day. Later in his reign, Seti promoted Paser, son of the high priest of Amun and one of Ramesses's close companions, to vizier. This appears to have been a wise choice. Like Seti, Paser was driven by a vision of Egypt's golden age. The biography in his tomb states, "Let it be made just like that of ancient times."[i]

---

[i] Nielsen, Nicky. *Pharaoh Seti I: Father of Egyptian Greatness.* Pen & Sword History, Barnsley, 2018.

Seti I took Sinai and added it to Egypt and then advanced as far as Damascus to the north. However, he was unable to attack the Hittites in their seat of power, as there was unrest in Libya and western Egypt that he had to attend to. As a northerner, Seti knew the Nile Delta well, and he created a new royal palace at Avaris (Hut-Waret), the former Hyksos capital on the eastern side of the delta. This wasn't just a holiday home in his old country; it became a major marshaling camp for campaigns to the east and north, and large-scale metalworking facilities were installed there, enabling the mass production of weapons.

A fort at Tjaru, on the road north into Palestine, was built to protect Egypt's access to the area. A second campaign to the north secured the city of Kadesh, where Seti set up a stela to celebrate his conquest. Seti also built forts in Nubia to the south and Libya to the west.

In Nubia, Seti faced a rebellion from Egypt's old enemy. Rather than using brute force and attacking the forces based in desert oases, he sat things out in his fortresses, forcing the enemy to come to him. When they did, they found themselves trapped with no access to water. Here, just as in Palestine, Seti was able to consolidate what had become fragile Egyptian territories.

At the same time, Seti began building. He reopened the quarries of Gebel el-Silsila and Aswan to provide sandstone and granite for his building program. He completed the great hypostyle hall at Karnak, with its huge papyrus-shaped columns and raised relief scenes showing his victories. The figure of his son Ramesses appears, fighting together with him in the reliefs; however, just as you cannot trust everything you read in the newspapers, you cannot trust everything you see carved on a temple wall. Ramesses actually re-cut the reliefs to include his name, effectively Photoshopping himself into the battle.

Seti created a mortuary temple for himself at Luxor at a slightly unusual site in Gurna, which was farther north than most of the mortuary temples but on the processional route connecting Karnak with the temples of Mentuhotep and Hatshepsut at Deir el-Bahri. This was the route of the procession of Amun during the Beautiful Festival of the Valley. Seti gave the temple a heavily fortified enclosure wall, harkening back to the enclosures of the first dynasties, and built a palace adjacent to the front court. Art during Seti's reign was delicately cut in raised reliefs; it was a high point of Egyptian art, though it was undeniably more conservative than the art of the Amarna years.

Seti I's tomb was one of the biggest and deepest ever built in the Valley of the Kings. It was also one of the most decorated. Its eleven chambers have their ceilings painted with gold stars on a blue background, with decorations including the Litany of Ra, which shows the pharaoh united with the sun god passing through the night to the morning. There are also scenes from the Amduat, the crucial New Kingdom "map" of the afterlife, and the "opening of the mouth" ritual, as well as numerous portrayals of Seti with various gods. However, the tomb was evidently robbed at some point. Seti's mummy was found in the cache at Deir el-Bahri, where the priests had taken it for safekeeping. His alabaster sarcophagus was brought to London in 1821, and it was refused by the British Museum, which thought it was too expensive at £2,000 (today close to $2.5 million). Instead, it was bought by an architect named Sir John Soane, who installed it in his house in London, where it can still be seen today.

Even though the tomb had been robbed, seven hundred of the pharaoh's shabtis were found when it was excavated in 1917. Evidently, Seti did not plan to do any work in the next life!

Seti built a huge temple at Abydos, which he named "Menmaatre happy in Abydos," together with a sunken tomb behind the temple called "Menmaatre beneficial to Osiris" (known today as the Osireion). This was not the tomb in which Seti's body would be buried, but a cenotaph asserting Seti's identity with Osiris was placed there. It was built in an archaic style, perhaps copying Khafre's valley temple at Giza.

The temple at Abydos is extremely innovative. Its two hypostyle halls lead to not one but seven sanctuaries for Osiris, Isis, Horus, Amun-Re, Re-Horakhty, Ptah, and the deified Seti. Behind those sanctuaries, accessed by a narrow passage, are halls and chapels devoted to the cult of Osiris. Another set of rooms is found on one side, giving the temple an odd L-shape, with chapels dedicated to Ptah and Nefertem and a gallery containing a king list.

The king list is interesting. It starts with "Menes" (Narmer) and runs all the way to Seti I, who is shown adoring the cartouches of his predecessors. In the same gallery, young Ramesses is shown as a youth wearing the sidelock of a child. (Egyptian children had their heads shaved except for a side plait.) Seti and Ramesses are lassoing a wild bull, a symbol of the pharaoh's domination of the wild and chaos.

We can only speculate what Seti could have achieved if he had been given another decade. However, he appears to have died suddenly after only a reign of just ten to fifteen years. Unlike his father and son, who both lived to be a ripe old age, Seti was not yet forty when he became one with Osiris. (Incidentally, the embalmers messed up this pharaoh too; they took out his heart by mistake and then sewed it back in on the wrong side.)

Seti made a return in the 20th century when an Englishwoman, Dorothy Eady, started having vivid dreams of him. She ended up in Egypt, where she became a draftswoman working for archaeological teams. She eventually settled in Abydos to be close to Seti. While it's easy to address her story as that of an eccentric and slightly crazed woman, many Egyptologists had a high regard for her, and she often demonstrated an uncannily accurate knowledge of where to dig.

Seti missed greatness so narrowly. His son Ramesses, on the other hand, became Ramesses the Great. He was also known as Usermaatre Setepenre (from which the Greek name "Ozymandias" was derived). Again, Ramesses took the name of Maat as part of his titulary, although with a rather more aggressive meaning: "The truth of Ra is powerful."

Professor Nicky Nielsen calls Ramesses "a young ruler in a hurry." He was certainly someone who paid a great deal of attention to public relations. Seti groomed him for power, giving him charge of the granite excavations and having him lead a Nubian campaign in his ninth year of ruling. This gave Ramesses experience as both a builder and a warrior, the pharaoh's two major tasks. However, he was not a vizier to his father, nor did Seti make him a co-ruler; perhaps Seti would have done so in due course had he not died. So, Ramesses had relatively little in-depth experience by the time he became pharaoh.

The Ramesside dynasty was determined to avoid a repeat of the Amarna revolution; it tended to be conservative and respectful of paternal relations. On the surface, Ramesses conformed to this pattern. He completed his father's works both at Abydos and in the hypostyle hall at Karnak.

However, when Ramesses looked at the reliefs in the hypostyle hall, he found them wanting. Seti was there, but where was Ramesses? Fortunately for him, it was a simple job to replace the figure of loyal troop captain Mehy with his own, and on the new walls he'd completed, he was able to show himself off to his advantage.

Ramesses also took his father's summer palace at Avaris and rebuilt it as his new capital, Pi-Ramesses or Per-Ramesses ("House of Ramesses").

The city was splendid. It was also decorated by at least fifty colossal statues of Ramesses. Eleven more colossi (at least) were also set up at Memphis, where Ramesses rebuilt the temple of Ptah. At the Luxor Temple, Ramesses not only finished Amenhotep III's work but also put another series of colossal statues of himself across the front of the temple. You couldn't enter without seeing the king.

Ramesses must have had the quarries working overtime. However, his building program was also a recycling project. He used Akhenaten's great capital of Akhetaten as a source of stone, demolishing this heretical legacy while creating his own monuments at the same time.

So, Egypt had three "capitals" of sorts: Memphis, home of the bureaucracy; Thebes, the religious capital; and Pi-Ramesses, the king's residence and possibly also his military headquarters. This didn't last. The Nile Delta is unstable land, and the branch of the Nile on which Pi-Ramesses was located dried up. By the Twenty-first Dynasty, the city had been abandoned.

Ramesses increased Egypt's power. First, he staved off threats on the northern coast, where the Sherden had become a menace, raiding from the sea. Ramesses lay in wait and managed to capture a number of them. Then, he recruited them into his bodyguard. They must have looked quite splendid and very un-Egyptian with their horned helmets and big round shields.

He built a series of forts to the west, protecting the Nile Valley from the Libyan nomads. Zawyet Umm el-Rakham, west of today's Alexandria, was set up as a fort, but it also became a place for trading with Crete and the Levant. Ramesses knew Egypt's return to greatness needed commercial as well as military impetus.

Ramesses must have been quite happy with his diplomatic prowess. In the fourth year of his reign, he managed to persuade the ruler of Amurru (northern Lebanon) to switch his allegiance from the Hittites to Egypt. However, this gave the Hittite king, Muwatalli, who had, at some point, retaken Kadesh from Egypt, an excuse to declare war. With 2,500 chariots and nearly 40,000 infantrymen, he was a force to be reckoned with.

The next year, Ramesses rode east with twenty thousand men, which were divided into four troop divisions: Amun, Re, Ptah, and Seth. He left his elite squad in Amurru to march on Kadesh in a classic pincer movement.

The Battle of Kadesh was a great Egyptian victory; well, at least if you believe Ramesses's story. He showed the battle scene at Karnak at the Ramesseum (twice), Abydos (twice), and Luxor (three times).

However, Hittite records suggest that Ramesses miscalculated. Believing two Hittite deserters who were caught by his scouts and said that Muwatalli had fled, Ramesses marched on Kadesh before checking the story out thoroughly and without bringing his full forces up. As it turned out, Muwatalli was waiting for him in front of the walls of Kadesh. The Re division, which had advanced first, fled the field, leaving Ramesses alone with only the Amun division to protect him. The Ptah and Seth divisions had not yet arrived on the battlefield.

Ramesses waited until the Hittite soldiers stopped to plunder the Egyptian camp and then immediately counterattacked with his chariots. The counterattack was successful for a while, but Muwatalli led another attack against Ramesses. However, the elite troops from Amurru arrived at that point, rescuing Ramesses from his tactical mistake of engaging his troops before bringing up his full strength.

The next day, according to Ramesses, the Hittites sued for peace. However, Ramesses did not sign a treaty and didn't even attempt to capture the city of Kadesh. The Hittites soon recovered their influence in the area, and several local kings were tempted to try their luck by withholding tribute they owed the pharaoh, leading to a number of punitive campaigns. To the unbiased observer, it looks as if Ramesses was lucky not to be heavily defeated by the wily Muwatalli, though he displayed great personal courage in fighting his way out of a tricky situation.

Looking at the multiple retellings of the Battle of Kadesh, one shouldn't forget that the theme of a pharaoh "smiting the foreigner" goes all the way back to the Narmer Palette; it's a standard theme of the pharaoh fulfilling his duty to preserve Maat and hold back the forces of chaos. Very often, it's the image that is used on the pylon that gives access to the temple so that it marks the border between the temple, the domain of Maat, and the secular world.

Later on in Ramesses's reign, after the death of Muwatalli, the Hittite king's son, Urhi-Teshub (or Mursili III) was deposed. He sought refuge at the Egyptian court. This time, diplomacy rather than war was successful. In Ramesses's twenty-first year of rule, a peace treaty was inscribed on two silver tablets, giving Egypt free access to the port of Ugarit and firm control over Egyptian vassals in the Levant. Hattusili remained in place and also sent a daughter as a bride for Ramesses.

Ramesses had already created a huge harem. Pharaohs had always been polygamous, unlike almost all of their subjects, but the number of wives seems to have increased markedly in the Nineteenth Dynasty. Ramesses married his first wife, Nefertari, before he became pharaoh. At Abu Simbel, Ramesses built a temple in her name next to his own and showed her as the same size as himself. This was unprecedented. In fact, the only temple previously dedicated to a Great Royal Wife had been dedicated by the heretic Akhenaten to Nefertiti.

Nefertari had at least four sons and two daughters, and her successor as Great Royal Wife, Isetnofret, had three sons and a daughter. However, this pales beside the total list of Ramesses's progeny. Ramesses was one of the first pharaohs to show a complete list of all his children in his temples, including both sons and daughters. There were between 88 and 103 in total. (Sons were very rarely shown before this date unless they were co-rulers or held another important office.) Ramesses emphasized his fertility, partly because it was linked to the fertility of Egypt itself but also because he perhaps wanted to show that he had enough legitimate sons to avoid a succession crisis like what happened after the reign of Akhenaten.

Neither Nefertari nor Isetnofret were King's Daughters. However, after Isetnofret's death, Ramesses appears to have taken the decision to stick with tradition and marry the daughter of a pharaoh. However, the only King's Daughters available, apart from foreign princesses, were his own daughters. He married at least three of them: Bintanath, Meritamen, and Nebettawi. He also married two Hittite princesses as a result of the peace treaty with Hattusili.

Ramesses reigned for a total of sixty-six years. He celebrated his Sed festival after thirty years, which was a rare achievement, and then continued to hold Sed festivals every few years. He held more than a dozen Sed festivals in total. He died at around the age of ninety. Ramesses had bad teeth and terrible arthritis. He used henna to turn his white hair back to the flaming red he'd inherited from Seti. His tomb, KV7, had been completed within a dozen years after his accession; it had been waiting for him a long time.

However, he had also built KV5, a most unusual tomb with over 130 chambers; it was the largest single tomb in the entire Valley of the Kings. It was located near Ramesses's tomb and has been excavated by American

Egyptologist Kent Weeks. This catacomb held the burials of most of Ramesses's children, keeping the family together after death. (It is, in some ways, similar to the Serapeum, a tomb at Saqqara built for the holy Apis bulls. It was built by one of Ramesses's sons, Khaemwaset).

Ramesses's building works are immense: his mortuary temple at Luxor, which shows his own version of the divine birth myth created by Hatshepsut; the huge cliff-cut temple complex of Abu Simbel in Nubia; works at Luxor Temple and at Karnak; and a number of monuments farther south in Nubia.

Four huge statues of Ramesses guard the temple of Abu Simbel, seen as it was before 1923. [51]

But Ramesses's work is less delicate and fine than Seti's. Perhaps the pace of construction meant the best carvers were always overworked. The difference can be clearly seen in the temples that Ramesses took over from his father (Gurna, Karnak, and Abydos). Seti's work is in delicate raised reliefs; the stone was cut away, leaving the figures standing proud. Ramesses's work appears to have thick black borders. They are sunken reliefs, where the outlines are cut out deeply to "sink" the figures into the stone. Because the whole background doesn't have to be cut away, it's much faster to carve. It's also—and this might have appealed to Ramesses, who had "Photoshopped" his way into Seti's battle scenes—much more difficult to erase.

By the way, you should remember that despite the sophisticated structure of Egyptian society at this time, Egypt was still in the Late Bronze

Age. Temples were built using stone hammers and copper or bronze chisels, saws, and drills. There was still very little iron available, mainly because the Hittites had it all, making it a luxury material in Egypt.

Despite Ramesses's impressive fertility, he lived so long that many of his children died before him. In the end, it was his thirteenth son, Merneptah, who succeeded him. By that time, Merneptah was already nearly seventy.

After Ramesses the Great, the Nineteenth Dynasty is something of an anticlimax. Ramesses III built the temple at Medinet Habu in Luxor, next to the Ramesseum, and tried to model himself on his hero, Ramesses the Great, who had died fifty years prior. But times had changed. Where Ramesses the Great had fought to expand Egypt, Ramesses III's wars were all defensive.

Ramesses III had bad luck at home too. First, he had to head off a workers' strike at Deir el-Medina after wheat deliveries to the village were delayed. Then, there was a harem conspiracy that aimed at replacing him with his son Pentawere. There was a trial; all the main conspirators were executed or committed suicide. Ramesses III, though, was dead. His mummy shows a deep and lethal cut to the throat, and his left big toe had been chopped off as well (and nicely replaced by a prosthesis during the mummification process).

Ramesses IV succeeded his father, and there was a line of more Ramesses, going all the way to Ramesses XI. However, the Nile inundations grew ever lower, rendering the country less fertile, and there was corruption and civil unrest. Tax revenues fell. Ramesses VI couldn't afford to build at Karnak, so he just had his own name carved on Ramesses IV's work.

Tomb robbing had become a common practice, and even officials were involved in the thievery; even the temple of Karnak was robbed. Meanwhile, state offices had become practically hereditary. Ramessesnakht was the high priest of Amun under six pharaohs and was succeeded by his son Amenhotep.

By the end of the dynasty, there was a civil war. The Nubian viceroy Panehsy installed himself in Thebes. Piankh, the general detailed to deliver Thebes, decided to rule the city himself after he took it and indulged in tomb robbing to finance his government. Egypt was once again divided.

Chapter 7: Mysteries of the Mummies: Death and Afterlife of the Pharaohs

In the British Museum's Egyptian galleries, there is a low glass case. Inside it is a reconstructed sand grave that dates from before the pharaohs. In it, a naked, ginger-haired man lies curled up on one side, surrounded by terracotta pots.

This mummy dates from around 3400 BCE and was one of a number found by E. A. Wallis Budge at the end of the 19th century. "Ginger" was mummified naturally by the sand piled around his body, which is still in remarkably good condition. The curled position is found in pre-dynastic and early dynastic burials; burying bodies fully stretched out was not typical until the Fifth Dynasty. But from 3400 BCE onward, mummification became the defining characteristic of Egypt, setting it apart from the cultures around it.

The myth of Isis and Osiris was central to Egyptian ideas of mummification. Seth, Osiris's evil brother, created a chest to Osiris's measurements and promised to give it to whoever could fit in it exactly. When Osiris got in, Seth locked him up and sent the chest out to sea. It washed up in Lebanon, where a cedar grew around it. When the cedar was felled, it was used as a pillar in the Lebanese king's palace.

Osiris's wife, Isis, dreamed of the pillar in the palace and was able to reclaim the body. Seth had to prevent Osiris from being reborn, so he hacked the body into pieces and scattered them throughout Egypt. Isis found the pieces and was able to bring Osiris back to life, which allowed her to give birth to a son, Horus.

The important thing in this myth is the idea that the body must be preserved and made holy for the soul to live. The sacred nature of the mummy was even more important than the intact state of the body. For instance, on the north side of Sneferu's Meidum Pyramid, a wooden box that contained a de-fleshed body and another body that had each joint wrapped separately was found. These were in no way intact, but they had been treated in a ritualistic way.

Many scholars believe that the earliest mummies were naturally created. However, analysis of remains in the Turin Egyptian Museum in Italy, which come from the same find as "Ginger," show that materials, including gum, resin, and aromatics, had been used on the body in a very similar way to later Egyptian processes. Deliberate mummification as part of the funerary ritual predates the pharaohs.

The style of mummification developed over the centuries. As early as the Second Dynasty, resins were used together with natron in vast quantities to desiccate the mummy and give it an impenetrable surface. Eventually, bodies were swathed in linen bandages to create a type of portrait statue. The exterior of the bandages was painted and sculpted to resemble the person in life. During the Pyramid Age, death masks were made, as well as "reserve heads" in limestone, which might have been intended to stand in for the original head if it was destroyed, or it might have magically assisted the mummy to regain its lifelike appearance.

The mummy of Ranefer, from the Fourth Dynasty, was modeled to look like a statue. The hair was painted black, and the eyebrows were green. The brain was intact, which appears to have been the case throughout the Old Kingdom. Unfortunately, this ancient mummy from Meidum was lost in the bombing of London during the Second World War.

By this time, bodies had begun to be eviscerated before mummification. Taking out the internal organs made the body easier to dry out. However, the later practice of taking out the brain was not employed until much later; we can tell because the ethmoid bone has to be broken for extraction to take place, and it is intact in the early mummies.

Until the Middle Kingdom, the arms, legs, and even individual fingers were separately wrapped. By the Twelfth Dynasty, canopic jars were used to enshrine the removed organs. The heart, though, was always left in the body. (In Seti I's case, it was taken out by mistake and then put back on the wrong side!) The Egyptians believed that the heart was the seat of thought and emotion. Since the heart would be weighed to decide whether the deceased was "justified," it was important to ensure it remained intact within the body. On the other hand, the brain, which was not considered important, was simply thrown away.

Things changed during the New Kingdom. The brain was always removed, and the body was immersed in a saline bath. Once dry, the mummy was anointed with a resinous paste or varnish. The crossed arm pose seen on Tutankhamun's inner coffin appears with Thutmose II, who also had his ears plugged with resin balls.

The New Kingdom was the heyday of mummification. Mummies' legs, arms, and necks were stuffed with resinous material to make them plump, as in life, and sunken eye sockets were packed with tiny linen pads. By the end of the Nineteenth Dynasty, even the cheeks were being packed, and artificial eyes were being used. Ramesses IV's mummy had small onions inserted as eyes.

By the end of the New Kingdom, the mummy had become a portrait statue. Herihor's wife, Nodjmet, had her cheeks and neck filled out. She was given artificial eyes, and her organs were wrapped in linen and repacked in her abdominal cavity. She was also painted with yellow ochre, the standard color in which women were shown in Egyptian art. Effectively, she had become a cult statue, something belonging to the realm of the gods.

Almost everything that is known about the actual process of mummification has been discovered by paying close attention to the mummies themselves. Egyptian texts describing mummification concentrate on the incantations that

The mummy of Great Royal Wife Nodjmet.[58]

were used during the process, not the anatomical proceedings.

By the New Kingdom, the process would be as follows. First, the body was washed and made clean. The brain would be extracted through the nose. Resin would be poured into the inside of the head to preserve it. A cut was made in the left (inferior) side of the body, and the internal organs were removed except for the heart. The internal cavity was washed with palm wine. The body's orifices were sealed with plugs of wax or linen. The body was then left either in a saline bath or under a heap of natron salt, which drew out all the moisture. This process would take around fifty days.

Once this had been done, the body would be anointed with resins. Myrrh and incense would be used to perfume the body, along with other aromatics; these were also used as offerings to the gods, so, again, the intention seemed to have been to turn the body into an object that could live in the world of the gods. Finally, the body was wrapped, which would take sixteen days, and was performed as a religious rite by the "master of secrets" and four priests. Amulets were placed in the wrappings, which were also painted with sacred texts.

Traditionally, it was thought that the body was preserved since the ka needed to inhabit it. However, it has been suggested that the many similarities between the creation of mummies and the creation and worship of divine images reflect a concept of the mummy as a sacred ritual object. In both cases, ritual purity was important, and in both cases, wrapping with many layers of linen was used. Linen wraps protected many of the statues in Tutankhamun's tomb, and they would have covered cult statues too. (Chantress Henattawy, whose coffin is in the Metropolitan Museum, was wrapped but not mummified.)

Wrapping would have had special meaning in a culture that was all about enclosure. Temples had no windows in the holy of holies and were surrounded by high mudbrick walls. Tutankhamun was buried in three coffins inside four shrines, and each coffin was shrouded (wrapped).

The stiffening of the skin during mummification made it resemble metal—a sign of eternity. It's interesting that Seti I's shabtis were coated with resin; the black varnish was a symbol of life after death, and it was also the same type of resin that was used in the mummification process. The use of ochre in many cultures was reserved for rituals. And the "opening of the mouth" rite performed on the mummy before its entombment was the same rite that was performed on statues of the gods.

In 2021, a huge procession of pharaohs' mummies was held in Cairo as they were transferred from the old Cairo Museum to the new National Museum of Egyptian Civilization. Almost all these mummies came from a single discovery made in 1881 by Gaston Maspero, the head of antiquities in Egypt, in a crack in the cliff between Deir el-Bahri and Gurna. Maspero summed up what fascinates most people about these mummies: "I still wonder if I am not dreaming when I see and touch what were the bodies of so many famous personages of whom we never expected to know more than the names."[i]

Mummies up to five centuries old had been taken from their tombs, reverently re-wrapped, and buried together with the high priests of Amun. For Ramesses the Great, this was his third tomb; he had already been reburied once, in the tomb of his father Seti I. A second cache of mummies was found in 1898 in the tomb of Amenhotep II, KV35.

In those days, unwrapping a mummy was treated as a spectacle. However, scientific study of the mummies has vastly increased our understanding of ancient Egypt. For instance, we know that tattooing and circumcision were practiced. We know that most Egyptians of any age had bad teeth, worn down from the gritty bread they ate, and that many of the pharaohs had bad arthritis.

Even after Egypt became Christian, bodies continued to be preserved in salt before being given a Christian funeral. Eventually, though, the practice died out.

But now it's making a comeback, thanks to curious Egyptologists! In 1994, Egyptologist Bob Brier worked with anatomist Ronn Wade at the University of Maryland to mummify a cadaver using original techniques and materials. In 2011, the University of York mummified a taxi driver called Alan Billis, who now resides in the Gordon Museum of Pathology, King's College, London.

---

[i] Riggs, Christina. *Unwrapping Ancient Egypt*. Bloomsbury, London, 2014.

Chapter 8: The Late Period and the End of Pharaonic Rule

Despite the Ramesside dynasty's striving for stability, the New Kingdom eventually collapsed. It's important not to see this as purely an internal, domestic issue. In fact, the Third Intermediate Period marked a major change in Egypt's status.

Up to the time of Ramesses II, Egypt was the center of its world. After about 1000 BCE, Egypt became a peripheral state and then ultimately a state dependent on greater powers, such as the Persians, Greeks, Romans, and even Libyans and Nubians, the latter two having been former subject peoples to the Egyptians. Other empires had fully entered the Iron Age; however, Egypt was still in the Bronze Age, giving it a technological handicap.

Egypt was also fragmented, with several dynasties based in the Nile Delta that had little power over the south of the country. Upper Egypt became increasingly independent. At Thebes, the high priests of Amun held greater power than many pharaohs of the age, even writing their names in cartouches.

This was an age of recycling. The Twenty-first Dynasty at Tanis, in the eastern Nile Delta, took apart the city of Pi-Ramesses, which was no longer viable after its branch of the Nile silted up. Even pharaonic tombs were recycled. Psusennes I was buried in the stolen sarcophagus of Merneptah, and his councilor Wendjebaendjedet was buried with a ring stolen from the tomb of Ramesses IX. (It's intriguing that the glories of the tomb included a silver coffin; in Egypt, silver was rarer and more expensive than gold.)

The Libyans, who were old enemies of Egypt, took over the kingdom with the Twenty-second and Twenty-third Dynasties. They had Libyan birth names, such as Shoshenq, Osorkon, and Takelot, but took Egyptian throne names. Osorkon IV deliberately took the same name as Ramesses the Great, Usermaatre.

Shoshenq I was a man of vision. He was not born into the royal family but gained his entry by marrying his son to Psusennes II's daughter and then took the throne upon the old pharaoh's death. He underpinned his position by making his son both the army commander and the high priest of Amun before setting out to make Egypt great again.

Egypt was becoming something of a joke internationally. Shoshenq set out on a tour of the Middle East, conquering Gaza, taking Megiddo, and extorting plunder from Jerusalem. He went back to Thebes, where he started a huge program of works at Karnak. He could have been another Ramesses the Great, yet he's almost unknown. That is because he died suddenly, and his successors had none of his vision or vigor.

By the Twenty-fifth Dynasty, Egypt was under the control of its ancient enemies, the Nubians. Kush had risen like a phoenix after the disintegration of the New Kingdom, and it had been thoroughly Egyptianized. Kush became independent, with its capital at Napata. Kings Alara and Kashta consolidated the kingdom, and Kashta's son, Piye, decided to invade Egypt. The Nubians adopted the cult of Amun after the Thutmosid pharaohs introduced it, and they appeared to have seen themselves as preservers of "real" Egyptian values.

Piye allowed the relatives of Osorkon IV to remain at Thebes, including God's Wife of Amun Shepenwepet, but he made sure that his daughter, also named Shepenwepet, would be her successor. He took the same throne name as Ramesses the Great, Usermaatre, and consolidated control of all of Egypt except for the Nile Delta. At one point, there were five separate kings in Egypt—Osorkon IV, Iuput II, Nimlot, Peftjauawybast, and Piye—but only Piye took the title of "dual king."

Piye was a fine horseman. When he took the rebellious Nimlot's capital of Khmun in the Nile Delta, he didn't even look at the women but went straight to the stables. After preserving Egypt's purity from the Libyans, he never bothered actually ruling Egypt. Instead, he went straight back to Napata.

The birth names of all these pharaohs were Nubian: Shebitku, Shabaka, Taharqa, and Tantamani. However, they were obsessed with Egypt's past, going back to the Old Kingdom for inspiration. They restored Memphis as the capital and even copied the heavy, squat, muscular style of Egyptian sculpture. When they built temples, they showed the Nubians as enemies being smited even though they were Nubians themselves.

They did not follow one important Egyptian custom. These rulers were buried near Jebel Barkal in Nubia, not in Egypt. However, when they built their Nubian tombs, they brought back the pyramid. There were more pyramids in Nubia than there ever were in Egypt.

Eventually, the Nubians were driven out of Egypt, although not by the Egyptians. The eastern kingdom of Assyria attacked. In 671 BCE, Taharqa was defeated by Esarhaddon of Assyria. Though Egypt successfully revolted, Esarhaddon's son, Ashurbanipal, reoccupied Egypt and plundered Thebes.

The Saite dynasty (the Twenty-sixth Dynasty), based at Sais in the Nile Delta, saw an opportunity in all of this disorder. Psamtik took the throne, and the Saites who followed changed course to try to follow the prevailing wind, allying first with Assyria and then later with the Greek civilization. Egypt was no longer setting the trends; it was following them.

Meanwhile, far to the east, Cyrus succeeded in gainng the throne of Persia. He then claimed the Median Empire and conquered Babylon and Anatolia, creating a Middle Eastern superpower. When Pharaoh Ahmose III died in 526 BCE, Cyrus's successor, Cambyses, saw this as an opportunity to add Egypt to the Persian Empire. Unlike almost all the other non-Egyptian kings, Cambyses only took three royal names, a Horus, throne, and birth name—Sematawy Mesutra Kembud, "uniter of the Two Lands, son of Ra, Cambyses." Some of the later Persians never even took a Horus name.

Greece began to put pressure on Persia, giving Egypt a chance to fight back. Amyrtaeus, a descendant of the Saite kings, led a successful revolt against the Persians in 404 BCE. He was a tragic pharaoh; his reign lasted just five years before he was defeated and executed by Nefaarud I. He was the only king of the Twenty-eighth Dynasty.

Egyptians could now see the pharaoh for what he was. The ruler was not a divine god-king but just a political opportunist. The Egyptian kingship had ceded its legitimacy. Within half a century, the Persians were back again, and this time, they didn't bother with throne names at all. Nectanebo II, the last native pharaoh, fled to Nubia.

There would only be three more Persian kings before a new pharaoh, who took the name of Setepenre Meryamun Aluksindres, blazed onto the scene. This man is not usually thought of as a pharaoh, though; he is much better known as a Macedonian conqueror. His name? Alexander the Great.

Alexander seemed to have had some kind of spiritual experience akin to some Westerners heading to an ashram in India. On his first visit to Egypt, he made a journey to the oracle of Amun in the Siwa Oasis. He went as a man and came back as a god. Alexander spent no more than a few months in Egypt, yet he's one of the pharaohs we know the most about as a character because he belonged to the Greek civilization, which had a rich history.

Alexander created a multicultural government with a Macedonian high command and two civil governors, one Persian and one Egyptian. When he died three years later, his general Ptolemy I Soter ("savior") decided to take the throne of Egypt. He not only took the same throne name as Alexander, but he also kidnapped Alexander's corpse to be buried first at Memphis and then in the new capital city of Alexandria.

Like many dynasties, the Ptolemies began well. Egypt turned toward the Mediterranean. Making the seaport of Alexandria the capital changed the way the empire thought of itself: it was a Mediterranean nation rather than "the gift of the Nile." Ptolemy I held Cyprus, and the next two Ptolemies added Anatolia, the Ionian coast, and southern Thrace, so that line of thought was natural. All of this made Egypt wealthy through trade. Ptolemy II reopened the canal that Darius had dug, a precursor of the Suez Canal, which gave Egypt a sea route to India. The result was a huge trading empire won by military might but driven by commerce. The Ptolemies turned Egypt into the breadbasket of their empire.

The Ptolemaic dynasty is paradoxical. By adopting the Egyptian custom of sibling marriage (though not polygyny), they kept the bloodline in their own family so that they were thoroughly Egyptian and Macedonian. They built new temples in Edfu, Kom Ombo, Dendera, and Esna that looked Egyptian. They also created the Library of Alexandria. For the Ptolemies, Athens was no longer the intellectual center of the Greek world; Alexandria was.

(The beginning of the Library of Alexandria was sordid. Ptolemy I borrowed books from Athenian libraries but didn't return them. The fines racked up, but as pharaoh, did he care?)

However, by the time of Ptolemy IV, things were already starting to go sour. Taxes were high, and Horwennefer and then Ankhwennefer rebelled in Upper Egypt. The Ptolemies were also losing their possessions outside Egypt, and an upstart civilization from Italy was beginning to threaten Greek hegemony in the Mediterranean.

The Ptolemies didn't help themselves, as they had a tendency to engage in family rivalry and internecine warfare. Ptolemy VI ruled alone at first but was forced to rule as part of a triarchy with his sister (and wife) Cleopatra II. Ptolemy VI was forced into exile in Rome by his younger brother, Ptolemy VIII, and then called back to Egypt. The two brothers ruled different parts of the empire, and when Ptolemy VI died, his brother ruled for nearly another twenty years.

("Where was Ptolemy VII?" you may well ask. It is not certain that he ever ruled at all, and he might have been awarded pharaonic status posthumously.)

An engraved portrait of Ptolemy VI showing the strange combination of Hellenistic art and Egyptian regalia.[58]

Ptolemy VIII took the incestuous nature of the royal house to new extremes. Co-ruling with his spouse and sister Cleopatra II, he then decided to marry his stepdaughter and niece, Cleopatra III (who was also, of course, his sister-wife's daughter). Historians have generally given him a bad name, and it seems undeniable that he was a psychopath. He had both his eldest sons (with Cleopatra II) killed to sideline them from the succession in favor of his children with Cleopatra III. He had waited many years to regain power, and he intended to enjoy it. He was brutal and pleasure-loving, but he was undeniably a shrewd politician.

Some of the history of Ptolemaic Egypt reads like a soap opera. Berenice III was the wife of and co-ruler with Ptolemy X. Her father, Ptolemy IX, deposed her husband, so she then co-ruled with him. Upon his death, she was forced to marry Ptolemy XI, her stepson, cousin, and likely also half-brother, who had her murdered two weeks afterward. This was not a particularly good move since the people of Alexandria were fonder of Berenice than they were of him. He was lynched in the gymnasium.

This left Egypt without a legitimate line of succession. Ptolemy XII, an illegitimate son of Ptolemy IX, relaunched the dynasty. He was nicknamed Ptolemy Auletes, the flute player. No one is sure whether that name came about because he played the flute or because he identified himself with the god Dionysus, whose followers played the flute (and drank to excess).

Rome continued to rise. It expanded throughout the Mediterranean, and ever since the rule of Ptolemy X, it had been extorting revenue from Egypt. (Ptolemy had offered the country as a deposit on the loan he'd needed for his civil wars.) The Romans were now talking openly about annexing Egypt, and Ptolemy XII was reduced to paying protection money.

Even so, he was forced out of Egypt in 58 BCE, and his daughter, Berenice IV, took over. She was a nasty piece of work. She married a cousin, Seleucus. After finding that he was not to her liking, she had him murdered within a week. Her next husband, a Greek officer in the Roman army, must have weighed the risks quite carefully before marrying her.

Ptolemy Auletes spent his exile in Rome, where Pompey hosted him; he might have taken his younger daughter with him. Rome would not support a coup on his behalf, but he borrowed money from a banker named Rabirius. The money was used to bribe general Aulus Gabinius (a friend of Pompey's). He acted, in effect, as a mercenary while also being a Roman governor.

Once Ptolemy XII was reinstalled, he executed his daughter Berenice and then made his Roman banker his finance minister. That only lasted a year, during which Rabirius squeezed as much as he could out of the country. Then, he was sent back to Rome. Egypt was now a major debtor, and just like the World Bank and the IMF today, the Romans were able to call the shots.

(By the way, Ptolemy Auletes finished off the new temple of Horus at Edfu and had himself portrayed there as a typical pharaoh, smiting the enemy, despite his lack of practice at enemy-smiting. The way pharaohs were portrayed had not changed since the time of King Narmer, though the political realities had.)

It was at this point that the last of the great pharaohs you'll recognize by name appears: Cleopatra VII, known as Weretnebetneferu Akhetzeh to her Egyptian subjects.

For most of her reign, Cleopatra was a co-ruler. She co-ruled with her father, Ptolemy XII, for just a year and then co-ruled with her brother and possible husband Ptolemy XIII, with her brother and husband Ptolemy XIV, and with her son Ptolemy XV. None of these Ptolemies ever had a play written about them or were the heroes of films. Cleopatra, on the other hand, has fascinated the ages.

She was forced into exile by Ptolemy XIII after crop failures and high inflation led to a recession. However, she was tough. She raised an army in Palestine and faced her brother in the Nile Delta. Ptolemy XIII decided to make a play for Julius Caesar's support by betraying Pompey, who had made for Egypt after being defeated by Caesar in Greece. Ptolemy thought Caesar would appreciate Pompey's severed head. Ptolemy was wrong, though; Caesar was not impressed.

Ptolemy also had underestimated his sister, who managed to gain access to Caesar's quarters. She was twenty-one, and Caesar was fifty-two. They were both big risk-takers, and one thing led to another. Ptolemy drowned in the Nile while battling his sister, and Cleopatra announced her younger brother, Ptolemy XIV, as co-regent. She was now the undisputed pharaoh, but three Roman legions were permanently stationed in Egypt. It had become a vassal state.

Cleopatra was perhaps the most Egyptian of the Ptolemies. She could actually speak the language of the land she ruled; as far as we know, none of the other Ptolemies could. (According to the Roman historian Plutarch, Cleopatra could also speak Ethiopian, Hebrew, Arabic, and Persian.) However, she decided to spend her time in Rome with her beloved Caesar rather than stay in Alexandria. This lasted for two years until Caesar's assassination in 44 BCE.

Cleopatra fled back to Egypt. Ptolemy XIV had conveniently died, so Caesarion, her three-year-old son with Caesar, became her co-ruler as Ptolemy XV. Cleopatra began to present herself as Isis, the divine mother with a divine son, the young Horus, "heir of the god who saves, chosen of Ptah, carrying out the Maat of Ra, living image of Amun."

But Cleopatra's reign was not prosperous. Low inundations led to food shortages. The Roman situation was fluid; a civil war had broken out after Caesar's death. Whether driven by emotion or by political calculation, she backed Mark Antony and Octavian, Caesar's supporters. She helped Mark Antony beat Caesar's assassins at the Battle of Philippi and managed to get him into bed (making him the second Roman general that she courted). She must have hoped that he would be the future ruler of Rome. She also managed to convince him to have her rebellious sister, Arsinoe, murdered.

Unfortunately for Cleopatra, this situation didn't last either. After Cleopatra gave birth to twins, Mark Antony left her, going back to Rome to marry Octavian's sister and renew the alliance with Octavian. It is quite possible that both he and Cleopatra believed this would leave Egypt well protected. They just had to put their personal feelings on the back burner to ensure their mutual safety. It didn't work.

Even though Cleopatra benefited from a run of good years for the Nile inundation and good harvests, Egypt was still paying off a huge amount of debt and struggling under the burden. Rome was bleeding Egypt dry. Antony fell out with Octavian over his plans to extend the empire eastward.

This time, Cleopatra's political acumen failed her, as she backed the wrong side. Antony's public rejection of his wife, Octavia, further damaged his relationship with Octavian. Soon, Octavian and Antony were at war.

Antony and Cleopatra sailed for Greece. (This could have never happened in pre-Ptolemaic Egypt since boats were once designed for sailing only on the shallow Nile.) There, they were blockaded at Actium. They found that Antony's land forces had defected, so they fled to Egypt. Back in Alexandria, they pretended nothing had happened.

However, they had run out of room. Before Octavian could get to Alexandria, Antony killed himself, supposedly after hearing that Cleopatra had committed suicide. Cleopatra locked herself in her already prepared tomb and killed herself upon hearing that Octavian proposed to take her to Rome in a triumph (a victory parade).

Caesarion escaped and was on his way to India when he was captured and executed. Alexander Helios, Cleopatra Selene, and four-year-old Ptolemy Philadelphus, Mark Antony and Cleopatra's children, were taken to Rome and displayed in Octavian's triumph. They were then given to Mark Antony's divorced wife, Octavia, to raise. Cleopatra Selene was eventually married to Numidian Prince Juba II, and they ruled Mauretania from their capital, Caesarea, in modern Algeria.

That is the story. The facts, of course, are susceptible to many different interpretations.

Who was Cleopatra? The trouble is that there are so few primary sources. Most of what we know about her was told by Roman, not Egyptian, historians, who, besides being biased, probably did not understand the Egyptian culture. Additionally, most of them were writing histories two hundred years after she lived. For other pharaohs, we depend on official inscriptions. Cleopatra left no letters or other documents.

As for what she looked like, perhaps the best witnesses are the coins minted for her, which show a woman with an aquiline nose, deep-set eyes, and a strong chin. She was not by any means a beauty if these coins are to be believed, but she was still a very striking woman. By contrast, most statues and reliefs show either an idealized Hellenic woman or an idealized Egyptian goddess, depending on the context and style of the work.

Octavian went on to found an empire. As Augustus, he created the Roman Empire, which would dominate most of Europe for five hundred years. However, he also killed an empire, for that was the end of Egypt.

Chapter 9: The Influence and Legacy of Ancient Egypt's Rulers

Egypt has changed greatly since the days of the pharaohs. After first becoming a Christian country (Coptic Christians still account for 10 to 15 percent of Egypt's population), Egypt was conquered by the Arabs in 640 CE and brought into the Muslim world. Today's Egypt has little in common with the Egypt of the pharaohs. Even the seasons have changed since the annual Nile inundations no longer happen, thanks to the erection of the Aswan Dam.

Nevertheless, ancient Egypt retains a powerful fascination. The Greek historian Herodotus (c. 484-425 BCE) was intrigued by the Egyptian culture and left us the first account of mummification; though, like many later travelers to Egypt, he seems to have found it difficult to distinguish fact from fiction.

Egypt left a massive monumental tradition, which became part of Western culture. Roman emperors carried obelisks from Egyptian temples to Rome, setting a precedent for later civilizations to follow. There are obelisks in Paris, London, and New York, as well as thirteen in Rome. The pyramids—with the Pyramid of Giza being the only one of the Seven Wonders of the Ancient World to survive—became famous and were copied around the world. There's even a pyramid on the US dollar bill, as well as the slightly under-life-sized pyramid at the Luxor Hotel in Las Vegas.

Perhaps more prosaic but equally important is the fact Egyptians started writing on papyrus. Other ancient civilizations used clay or stone as writing mediums. Egypt invented paper and ink (well, at least papyrus and ink). They also appeared to have invented math and the decimal system, as well as the ability to measure time through water clocks. This got passed on to the world through later civilizations, particularly the Greeks.

Even more important, Egypt developed a centralized economy and bureaucracy that was capable of organizing and sustaining large projects such as the pyramids, and they had a sophisticated method of taxation based on theoretical agricultural yields. In fact, Egypt probably invented job titles.

In agriculture, it's easy to dismiss the simple Egyptian ox plow and hoe as barely a step beyond the Stone Age. However, Egypt developed a unique form of agriculture because it was able to harness the Nile's inundation, refining its hydraulic methods over the centuries. For instance, the shaduf, a sort of see-saw for lifting water efficiently, was an Egyptian invention, and it is still used across the Middle East. The use of reserve ponds to retain floodwater for future use was another development that increased agricultural yields, and land reclamation on a large scale got started with the development of the Faiyum Oasis.

Egypt had an enduring influence on its age. Thanks to the new links between Egypt and Rome, the goddess Isis became one of the great gods of the Roman Empire. However, because the ability to read hieroglyphs and the more cursive Demotic and Hieratic Egyptian texts died out, the Egyptian culture ended up being represented only in the visual arts. The Egyptian culture was still impressive, but it was mysterious. Greece and Rome became the guiding lights of Western culture instead.

However, some access to Egyptian history was still possible through Greek and Roman texts. For instance, you may not immediately connect Seti I with Mozart, but a novel by the French writer Terrasson, *Sethos*, allowed Seti's name to become associated with philosophical ideas taken up by the Viennese Masonic lodge Zur wahren Eintracht, to which Mozart belonged. And while *Sethos* is a load of nonsense, the work Mozart based on it, *The Magic Flute*, is a masterpiece.

It wasn't until 1822 that French philologist Jean-François Champollion was able to decipher hieroglyphics by comparing the Greek and Egyptian texts carved on the Rosetta Stone. This discovery brought ancient Egypt back to life. Egyptian motifs were adopted in European and American architecture, and there was a further boost in the study of Egyptian culture when Tutankhamun's tomb was discovered in 1922. Four years after the discovery, the Carreras Tobacco Company built a London factory in the Art Deco Egyptian style, with black cats 1 guarding the door, papyrus-styled capitals, and an Egyptian cornice taken from Karnak.

The Carreras Tobacco Factory invokes the spirit of Tutankhamun.⁵⁴

Egypt became a huge resource for the imagination of creative artists. There were horror stories, such as "The Mummy's Curse," the tale of a mummy in the British Museum that was bad luck for anyone who photographed it (apparently apocryphal), and novels like Agatha Christie's *Death on the Nile* and Carter Dickson's *Curse of the Bronze Lamp*. Madame Blavatsky, a spiritual guru, blended ancient Egyptian mythology with Tibetan Buddhist and Hindu ideas.

Then, there was the pharaonic splendor of Egypt, which lent itself to film. *Land of the Pharaohs* (1955) dramatizes the building of the Great Pyramid of Giza; the movie is spectacular, though the story is rather silly. *Antony and Cleopatra* (1963), starring Elizabeth Taylor, won four Oscars, but it nearly bankrupted the film company.

More recently, French graphic novel writer Bilal has created a series in which ancient Egyptian gods land in Paris in 2023. Terry Pratchett brought humor to Egypt with his book *Pyramids*, and Neil Gaiman's *Sandman* features the Egyptian gods Anubis, Bastet, and Bes.

Afrocentrism has developed as an alternative way of viewing the world of the pharaohs. Many 19th-century archaeologists were obsessed with proving that the pharaohs were Caucasian instead of belonging to the "servile" African and Semitic races. A countercurrent has developed that claims the pharaohs of Egypt as part of a Black empire. While some of these claims have been overstated, the Egyptian culture certainly looks very African in some ways, with priests dressed in leopard skins, mother goddesses, and animal-headed gods looking like the masked figures of some African dance societies. The use of headrests for sleeping is also distinctively African.

In fact, while Egyptians were quite xenophobic, seeing themselves as surrounded by enemies, they appear to have been quite pragmatic about who was "Egyptian" in daily life. Being an Egyptian meant worshiping Egyptian gods and having an Egyptian name. The culture that developed in the Nile Valley was not a Middle Eastern culture; it was a distinct culture based on the unique conditions of living in the valley and not on any concept of race. But whatever the skin color or the precise DNA makeup of its inhabitants, it *was* a culture that was born in Africa.

Archaeologists are now discovering far more about the real world of ancient Egypt. Non-invasive scanning of mummies, aerial surveys, artificial intelligence, 3D scanning, and radar scans have all brought us new knowledge that wasn't previously available. New discoveries have been made at Saqqara in the last decade, and a respected Egyptologist has claimed that Nefertiti's tomb lies hidden behind a re-cut panel in Tutankhamun's tomb. Old mummies are being reassessed to give us new information, and even the food included in some of the tombs is being looked at again to see just what the Egyptians ate and drank. Renowned craft brewery Dogfish Head even worked with archaeologist Patrick McGovern to produce an ancient Egyptian beer, Ta Henket.

Ancient Egypt was a land of many secrets, and it hasn't given them all up yet.

Conclusion

This book has galloped through three thousand years of Egyptian history, from the pre-dynastic tombs of Abydos to the last pharaoh, Cleopatra VII. Egypt was the longest lasting empire in history thus far. The Roman Empire lasted a few centuries, the Byzantine empire lasted a little longer, and most modern nations trace their roots back only a few hundred years. Only the Chinese can claim as long of a history as a unified state.

Although theological concepts and the way the country was governed changed over the years, the rule of the pharaohs lasted as long as ancient Egypt, although it was admittedly adapted from time to time to admit co-rulership, female pharaohs, and even foreign pharaohs.

Some Egyptologists spend their lives trying to disentangle what exactly went on in the Third Intermediate Period or to identify pharaohs who appear only in later king lists and for whom there is no archaeological evidence. Egyptian history still has a lot of blanks to fill in. However, the overall outline of Egypt's history, particularly the place of its greatest pharaohs, is clear.

From Narmer, who united the Two Lands, to the great builders (Djoser, Khufu, and Khafre) to the great Seti I and Ramesses II, Egypt was the prevailing power. The Egyptians could afford to look at foreigners with contempt. The Egyptians knew how to write, how to build immense temples, and how to do math. Admittedly, timber had to be imported, and some foreigners produced interesting luxury goods, but for the most part, Egypt had a highly defined sense of nationhood. While other cultures of its time, such as Assyria, Babylon, Mitanni, and the Hittite Empire, rose and fell and had to compete with other kingdoms, Egypt remained unified, even under foreign rulers.

It was only with the Persian conquest that Egypt became a colonized country. By this time, its technologies were no longer advanced. Other civilizations had developed their own alphabets and structures of governance, and they had grabbed the opportunities of the Iron Age with both hands. Meanwhile, Egypt, with no natural sources of iron, was left scrabbling to stay afloat. The rise of Greece and then Rome left Egypt as a backwater; it was a huge producer of grain and tax revenues for the Roman Empire, but it was not much more than that.

Egypt is still fascinating, both for the amazing monuments it left behind and for some of its humblest and most intimate remains, such as a toy lion that opens its mouth to roar (in the British Museum) or a beaded dress for a dancer (in the Petrie Museum, London). It seems amazing that we can get so close to people who lived such a long time ago. And yet, in some ways, we'll never know them, particularly the pharaohs. They were so hedged in with artistic conventions, political necessities, and religious duties that most of what was written about them was purely ritualistic. It took a very strong pharaoh to make his (or her) mark; fortunately, Egypt had a few strong rulers.

If you've read this book attentively, you should have a good grasp of Egypt's history and the major rulers who made the country what it was. You'll certainly notice future announcements of new discoveries, such as the mummification workshops for humans and animals found at Saqqara in 2023 and the sarcophagus of Ramesses II's chancellor, Ptahemwia, found in 2022. Maybe you'll want to go to Egypt yourself or visit one of the many museums in Europe and the US with an Egyptian collection.

When you look at the way government works in the modern world, with a separate treasury, different departments, and bureaucrats working away in their cubicles, remember that this was one of the inventions the ancient Egyptians left us. They might not have had a democracy, but they did have a very good administrative system.

Studying ancient Egypt is particularly interesting because it's a civilization that went through several periods of turbulence. Assessing the reasons why dynasties fell and why Egypt split apart during its three Intermediate Periods gives us plenty of clues on what to avoid if we want to continue living in a stable world. Meanwhile, looking at the great pharaohs who restored order, like Ahmose, Seti I, and Ramesses II, is an objective lesson in leadership.

These pharaohs might have lived as long as five thousand years ago, but they still have a lot to teach us today.

Pharaohs, Dynasties, and Dates

Any attempt at dating or even defining who were "real" pharaohs and who weren't is fraught with difficulty and even controversy. Some pharaohs are known by Greek and Egyptian names or by throne names rather than birth names. Sometimes, it is difficult to reconcile the different names, particularly in the early period. Different king lists show different names; in some cases, pharaohs might be "double counted," as their birth names and throne names have been taken to represent different pharaohs. There were also a number of co-rulers during the New Kingdom and under the Ptolemies (a dynasty that seemed to have been created purely to confuse historians). And during the Intermediate Periods, dynasties often overlapped, with rival pharaohs ruling from different cities.

This table is provided in an attempt to provide a ready reference. It must be noted that the dates are not definitive and that different sources provide different dates depending on which chronology they use.

Dynasty, Pharaoh	Date	Events outside Egypt
First Dynasty		
Narmer / Menes	c. 3000 BCE	
Hor-Aha		c. 3000: Construction of Stonehenge
Djer		
Djet		
Merneith		
Den		
Adjib		
Semerkhet		
Qa'a	c. 2900	
Sneferka		
Second Dynasty		
Hotepsekhemwy		
Nebra		
Nynetjer		
Ba		

Dynasty, Pharaoh	Date	Events outside Egypt
Weneg-Nebty	c.2740	
Wadjenes		
Nubnefer		
Senedj		
Seth-Peribsen		
Sekhemib	c. 2720	
Neferkara I		
Nerferkasokar		
Horus Sa		
Khasekhemwy		
OLD KINGDOM **Third Dynasty**		
Djoser Netjerikhet	c. 2650	
Djoser-tety Sekhemkhet		
Sanakht		
Qahedjet		
Khaba		

Dynasty, Pharaoh	Date	Events outside Egypt
Huni		
Fourth Dynasty		
Sneferu	2613-2589	
Khufu / Cheops	2589-2566	
Djedefre		
Khafre	2558-2532	
Menkaure		
Shepseskaf		
Fifth Dynasty		
Userkaf	2496-2491	
Sahure		
Neferikare		
Neferefre		
Shepseskare		
Nyuserre		
Menkauhor		
Djedkare		

Dynasty, Pharaoh	Date	Events outside Egypt
Unas	2375-2345	
Sixth Dynasty		
Teti		2334: Foundation of the Akkadian Empire
Userkare		
Pepi I Meryre		
Nemtyemsaf I Merenre		
Pepi II Neferkare		
Nemtyemsaf II Merenre		
Netjerkare I		
FIRST INTERMEDIATE PERIOD **Seventh and Eighth Dynasties**		
Menkare	c. 2181	
Neferkare II		
Neferkare III		
Djedkare Shemai		
Neferkare IV		
Merenhor		

Dynasty, Pharaoh	Date	Events outside Egypt
Sneferka		
Nikare		
Neferkare V		
Neferkahor		
Neferkare VI		
Neferkamin Anu		
Qakare		
Neferkaure		
Neferkauhor		
Neferikare		
Ninth Dynasty		
Khety I		
Neferkare VII		
Khety II		
Imhotep		

Dynasty, Pharaoh	Date	Events outside Egypt
Tenth Dynasty (Lower Egypt)		
Meryhathor	2130	
Neferkare VIII		
Wahkare		
Merykare		
Eleventh Dynasty (Thebes)		
Intef the Elder (not pharaoh but founder of the dynasty)		
Mentuhotep I	2133	
Intef I		
Intef II		
Intef III		
MIDDLE KINGDOM **Eleventh Dynasty**		
Mentuhotep II	2060-2040	
Mentuhotep III		
Mentuhotep IV		

Dynasty, Pharaoh	Date	Events outside Egypt
Twelfth Dynasty		
Amenemhat I	1991-1962	
Senwosret I	1971-1929	
Amenemhat II	1929-1895	
Senwosret II	1897-1878	
Senwosret III	1878-1839	
Amenemhat III	1860-1814	
Amenemhat IV	1816-1807	
Sobekneferu		
SECOND INTERMEDIATE PERIOD **Thirteenth Dynasty**		
Sobekhotep I	1802-1800	c. 1800: *Epic of Gilgamesh* written; Hammurabi's legal code
Amenemhat Sonbef		
Nerikare		
Amenemhat V		
Amenemhat VI		

Dynasty, Pharaoh	Date	Events outside Egypt
Sewesekhtawy		
Sewadjkare I		
Sobekhotep II	c. 1780	
Renseneb		
Hor		
Sekhmrekhutawy Khabaw		
Djedkheperu		
Kay Amenemhat Sedjefakare		
Wegaf		
Userkare		
Smenkhkare		
Intef IV		
Seth Meribre		
Sobekhotep III		
Neferhotep I		
Sobekhotep IV		

Dynasty, Pharaoh	Date	Events outside Egypt
Sobekhotep V		
Sobekhotep VI		
Wahibre		
Ay I Merneferre		
Ini		
Sewadjkare II		
Sobekhotep VII		
Merkheperre		
Merkare		
Seheqenre Sankhptahi		
Fourteenth Dynasty (Canaanite, based at Avaris)		
Yakbim Sekaenre	1805-1780	
Ya'ammu Nubwoserre		
Qareh Khawoserre		
Ammu Aahotepre		
Sheshi Maaibre		
Nehesy Aaserre		

Dynasty, Pharaoh	Date	Events outside Egypt
Sewadjkare III		
Nebdjefare		
Fifteenth Dynasty (Hyksos)		
Salitis	c. 1650	
Khyan Seuserenre		
Apepi Nebkhepeshre		
Khamudi Hotepibre	1555-1544	
Sixteenth Dynasty (Thebes)		
Djehuti	c. 1650	
Sobekhotep VIII		
Neferhotep III		
Nebiryaw I		
Nebiryaw II		
Semenre		
Seuserenre		
Dedumose I		
Dedumose II		

Dynasty, Pharaoh	Date	Events outside Egypt
Montemsaf		
Mentuhotep VI		
Senwosret IV		
Seventeenth Dynasty (Upper Egypt)		
Rahotep	c. 1620	
Sobekemsaf I		
Sobekemsaf II		
Intef V		1600: Destruction of Minoan civilization by the Santorini eruption Mycenaean Greece rises to power
Intef VI		
Intef VII		
Ahmose I	c. 1558	
Seqenenre Tao	1558-1554	
Kamose	1554-1559	

Dynasty, Pharaoh	Date	Events outside Egypt
NEW KINGDOM **Eighteenth Dynasty**		
Ahmose II	1550-1525	
Amenhotep I	1541-1492	
Thutmose I	1520-1492	
Thutmose II	1492-1479	
Hatshepsut	1479-1458	
Thutmose III	1458-1425	
Amenhotep II	1425-1400	
Thutmose IV	1400-1390	
Amenhotep III	1390-1352	
Amenhotep IV / Akhenaten	1352-1336	
Smenkhkare		
Neferneferuaten		
Tutankhamun	1332-1324	
Ay	1324-1320	
Horemheb	1320-1292	

Dynasty, Pharaoh	Date	Events outside Egypt
Nineteenth Dynasty		
Ramesses I	1292-1290	
Seti I	1290-1279	
Ramesses II 'the Great'	1279-1213	
Merneptah	1213-1203	
Seti II	1203-1197	1200: Beginning of Hallstatt Celtic culture Bronze Age collapse in the Mediterranean and Middle East
Siptah	1197-1191	
Tawosret (probably the wife of Seti II)	1191-1190	
Twentieth Dynasty		
Setnakhte	1190-1186	
Ramesses III	1186-1155	
Ramesses IV	1155-1149	
Ramesses V	1149-1145	
Ramesses VI	1145-1137	

Dynasty, Pharaoh	Date	Events outside Egypt
Ramesses VII	1137-1130	
Ramesses VIII	1130-1129	
Ramesses IX	1129-1111	
Ramesses X	1111-110	
Ramesses XI	1107-1077	

THIRD INTERMEDIATE PERIOD
Twenty-first Dynasty (Tanis)

Nesbanebdjed I	1077-1051	
Amenemnisu	1051-1047	
Psusennes I	1047-1001	
Amenemope	1001-992	
Osorkon the Elder	992-986	
Siamun	986-967	
Psusennes II	967-943	

High priests of Amun (ruled but not crowned pharaoh)

Herihor	1080-1074	
Piankh	1074-1070	

Dynasty, Pharaoh	Date	Events outside Egypt
Pinedjem I Meriamun	1070-1032	
Masaharta	1054-1045	
Djedkonsuefankh	1046-1045	
Menkheperre	1045-992	
Nesbanadjed II	992-990	
Pinedjem II	990-976	
Psusennes III	976-943	
Twenty-second Dynasty (Libyan)		
Shosenq I	943-922	
Osorkon I	922-887	
Shosenq II	887-885	890: Homer writes the *Iliad* and *Odyssey*
Takelot I	885-872	
Osorkon II	872-837	
Shosenq III	837-798	814: Foundation of Carthage by the Phoenicians 800: Rise of the Greek city-states

Dynasty, Pharaoh	Date	Events outside Egypt
Shosenq IV	798-785	
Pami	785-778	
Shosenq V	778-740	776: First Olympic Games 753: Founding of Rome 745: Tiglath-Pileser III becomes king of Assyria and creates Assyrian Empire
Osorkon IV	740-720	
Twenty-third Dynasty (Libyan)		
Takelot II	837-813	
Pedubast I	826-801	
Iuput I	812-811	
Shosenq VI	801-795	
Osorkon III	795-767	
Takelot III	773-765	
Meriamun Rudamun	765-762	
Shosenq VII		

Dynasty, Pharaoh	Date	Events outside Egypt
Twenty-fourth Dynasty (Saite)		
Tefnakhte	732-726	
Bakenrenef	726-720	
Twenty-fifth Dynasty (Nubian or Kushite)		
Piye	744-714	
Shebitku	714-705	
Shabaka	705-690	
Taharqa	690-664	
Tantamani	664-653	
LATE PERIOD **Twenty-sixth Dynasty**		
Tefnakht II	685-678	
Nekauba	678-672	
Nekau I	672-664	
Psamtik I	664-610	612: Fall of Assyrian Empire
Nekau II	610-595	
Psamtik II	595-589	

Dynasty, Pharaoh	Date	Events outside Egypt
Wahibre	589-570	
Ahmose III	570-526	550: Cyrus founds Achaemenid Empire. Buddha and Mahavira (founder of the Jain religion) spread their ideas in India
Psamtik III	526-525	
Twenty-seventh Dynasty (Persian)		
Cambyses	525-522	
Darius	522-486	490: Battle of Marathon; Greeks defeat Persians
Xerxes	486-465	
Artabanus	465-464	
Artaxerxes	464-424	447-432: The Parthenon is built in Athens
Xerxes II	423	
Sogdianus	423	
Darius II	423-404	

Dynasty, Pharaoh	Date	Events outside Egypt
Twenty-eighth Dynasty		
Amyrtaeus	404-398	399: Death of Socrates; Plato writes an account of his death, as well as philosophical works
Twenty-ninth Dynasty		
Nefaruud I	398-393	
Hakor	392-391	
Pasherienmut	391	
Hakor (second reign)	390-379	
Nefaruud II	379	
Thirtieth Dynasty		
Nectanebo I	379-360	
Djedher	360-359	
Nectanebo II	359-340	
Thirty-first Dynasty (Persian)		
Artaxerxes III	340-338	
Artaxerxes IV	338-336	

Dynasty, Pharaoh	Date	Events outside Egypt
Darius III	336-332	
Argead Dynasty		
Alexander	332-323	
Philip Arrhidaeus of Macedon	323-317	
Alexander IV	317-309	
Ptolemaic Dynasty		
Ptolemy I Soter	305-285	
Ptolemy II Philadelphus	284-246	
Arsinoe II	277-270	
Ptolemy III Euergetes	246-222	
Berenice II	244-222	
Ptolemy IV Philopator	222-204	
Arsinoe III	220-204	
Ptolemy V Epiphanes	204-180	
Cleopatra I Syra	193-176	
Ptolemy VI Philometor	180-145	146: Rome destroys Carthage

Dynasty, Pharaoh	Date	Events outside Egypt
Cleopatra II	175-164: 163-127: 124-116	
Ptolemy VIII Physcon	171-163: 144-131: 127-116	
Ptolemy VII Neos Philopator	145-144	
Cleopatra III	142-131: 127-107	
Ptolemy Memphites	131	
Ptolemy XI Soter	116-110	
Cleopatra IV	116-115	
Ptolemy X Alexander	110-88	
Berenice III	81-80	
Ptolemy XI Alexander	80	
Ptolemy XII Auletes	80-58: 55-51	
Cleopatra V Tryphaena	79-68	71: Death of Spartacus 63: Rome takes Jerusalem
Cleopatra VI	58-57	
Berenice IV	58-55	

Dynasty, Pharaoh	Date	Events outside Egypt
Cleopatra VII	52-30	44: Assassination of Julius Caesar
Ptolemy XIII Theos Philopator	47	
Arsinoe IV	48-47	
Ptolemy XIV Philopator	47-44	
Ptolemy XV Caesarion	44-30	

Here's another book by Enthralling History that you might like

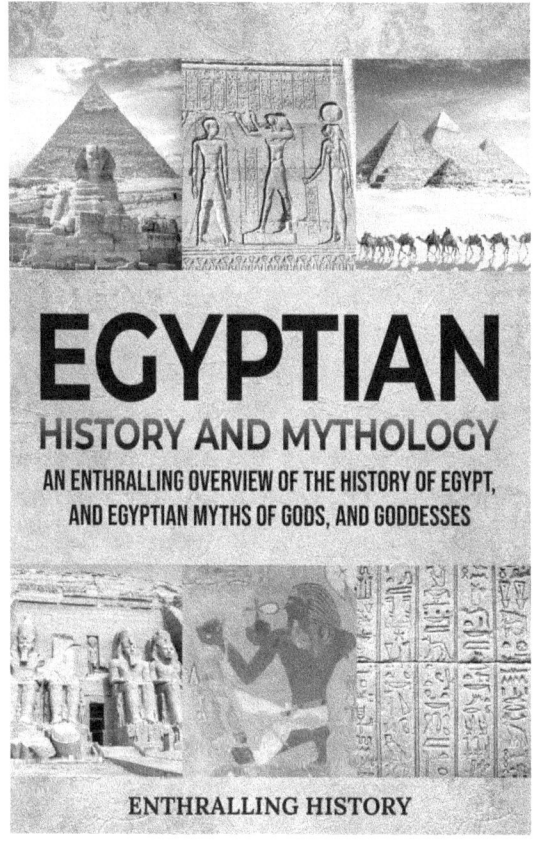

Free limited time bonus

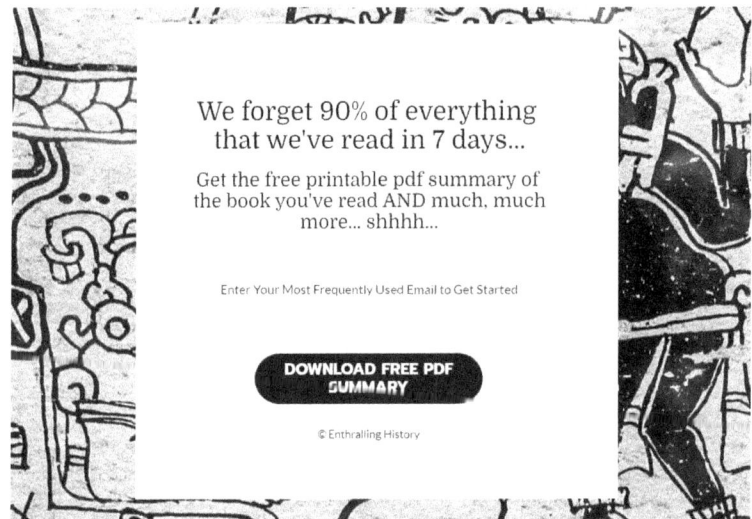

Stop for a moment. We have a free bonus set up for you. The problem is this: we forget 90% of everything that we read after 7 days. Crazy fact, right? Here's the solution: we've created a printable, 1-page pdf summary for this book that you're reading now. All you have to do to get your free pdf summary is to go to the following website:

https://livetolearn.lpages.co/enthrallinghistory/

Or, Scan the QR code!

Once you do, it will be intuitive. Enjoy, and thank you!

Bibliography

Part 1: Gods and Goddesses of Ancient Egypt

Anubis: the Jackal-Headed God of mummification and embalming. (2022, March 21). Timeless Myths.
https://www.timelessmyths.com/gods/egyptian/anubis/

Cult of Isis. (n.d.).
http://persweb.wabash.edu/facstaff/royaltyr/AncientCities/web/rel%20372%20project/ISIS.htm

Debeysklenar. (2021, July 23). *The Voyage of RA.* Debeysklenar.
https://debeysklenar.wordpress.com/2016/07/31/the-voyage-of-ra/

Egypt: Wadjet, Goddess of Lower Egypt, Papyrus, and Protector of Pharaoh. (n.d.). http://www.touregypt.net/featurestories/wadjeta.htm

Fawn, S. (2023, March 18). *Hymn to Nut, the Sky Goddess.* Iseum Sanctuary.
https://iseumsanctuary.com/2020/09/26/hymn-to-nut-the-sky-goddess/#:~:text=O%20Nut%2C%20cast%20yourself%20upon,one%20is%20among%20your%20children

Jackson, J. (n.d.). *Egyptian Myths.* Simon and Schuster.

Jerkins, M. (2021, January 4). *Lettuce and Kings: The power struggle between Horus and Set.* Michigan Quarterly Review.
https://sites.lsa.umich.edu/mqr/2015/05/lettuce-and-kings-the-power-struggle-between-horus-and-set-2/

Joe, J. (2022, January 11). *Babi: Get to know the monkey God of ancient Egyptian mythology.* Timeless Myths.
https://www.timelessmyths.com/mythology/babi/

Klimczak, N., & Klimczak, N. (2023, March 11). *Anubis, Egyptian God of the dead and the underworld.* Ancient Origins Reconstructing the Story of

Humanity's Past. https://www.ancient-origins.net/myths-legends/anubis-jackal-god-and-guide-ancient-egyptian-afterlife-006155

Mark, J. J. (2023). Anubis. *World History Encyclopedia.* https://www.worldhistory.org/Anubis/

Mark, J. J. (2023). RA (Egyptian God). *World History Encyclopedia.* https://www.worldhistory.org/Ra_(Egyptian_God)/

Mark, J. J. (2024). Great Female Rulers of Ancient Egypt. *World History Encyclopedia.* https://www.worldhistory.org/article/1040/great-female-rulers-of-ancient-egypt/

Mark, J. J. (2024). Serket. *World History Encyclopedia.* https://www.worldhistory.org/Serket/

Mark, J. J. (2024). Seshat. *World History Encyclopedia.* https://www.worldhistory.org/Seshat/

Mark, J. J. (2024). Horus. *World History Encyclopedia.* https://www.worldhistory.org/Horus/

Maydana, S. (2023, April 6). *The Contendings of Horus and Seth: Clash of the Egyptian Titans.* TheCollector. https://www.thecollector.com/contendings-horus-and-seth-egyptian-titans/

Nut - mythopedia. (n.d.). Mythopedia. https://mythopedia.com/topics/nut

Ogdoad of Hermopolis (Khmunu) | Ancient Egypt online. (n.d.). https://ancientegyptonline.co.uk/ogdoad/

Sobek | The Crocodile God of strength and power. (n.d.). https://www.ancient-egypt-online.com/sobek.html

Sullivan, K., & Sullivan, K. (2023, March 11). *The mythology of Nut, Mother of Gods.* Ancient Origins Reconstructing the Story of Humanity's Past. https://www.ancient-origins.net/myths-legends/mythology-nut-mother-gods-007084

Egyptian Mythology Creation Story. (2021, December 1). Egypt Tours Portal. https://www.egypttoursportal.com/en-us/the-creation-of-egyptian-mythology/

The story of RA and Isis. (2023, July 7). The Story Museum. https://www.storymuseum.org.uk/1001-stories/the-story-of-ra-and-isis

Winters, R., & Winters, R. (2019, September 3). *The Infinite Ogdoad: the creation pantheon of ancient Egypt and predecessor gods of the Old Kingdom.* Ancient Origins Reconstructing the Story of Humanity's Past. https://www.ancient-origins.net/human-origins-religions/infinite-ogdoad-creation-pantheon-ancient-egypt-and-predecessor-gods-old-020447

Part 2: Pharaohs of Ancient Egypt

Aldred, Cyril. *Akhenaten, Pharaoh of Egypt: A New Study.* Thames & Hudson, London, 1968.

Booth, Charlotte. *The Boy Behind the Mask: Meeting the Real Tutankhamun.* Oneworld, Oxford, 2007.

Brier, Bob. *The Murder of Tutankhamun: A True Story.* Putnam, 1998.

Cooney, Kara. *The Woman Who Would Be King: Hatshepsut's Rise to Power in Ancient Egypt.* Crown Publishers, New York, 2014.

David, Rosalie. *The Pyramid Builders of Ancient Egypt: A Modern Investigation of Pharaoh's Workforce.* Routledge & Kegan Paul, London, 1996.

Dodson, Aidan. *The First Pharaohs: Their Lives and Afterlives.* American University in Cairo Press, Cairo, 2021.

Jenkins, Nancy. *The Boat Beneath the Pyramid: King Cheops' Royal Ship.* Holt, Rinehart & Winston, New York, 1980.

Montserrat, Dominic. *Akhenaten: History, Fantasy and Ancient Egypt.* Routledge, London, 2000.

Nielsen, Nicky. *Pharaoh Seti I: Father of Egyptian Greatness.* Pen & Sword History, Barnsley, 2018.

O'Connor, David. *Abydos: Egypt's First Pharaohs and the Cult of Osiris.* Thames & Hudson, London, 2009.

Redford, Donald B. *Akhenaten: The Heretic King.* Princeton University Press, Princeton, 1984.

Riggs, Christina. *Unwrapping Ancient Egypt.* Bloomsbury, London, 2014.

Smith, Grafton Elliot and Dawson, Warren R. *Egyptian Mummies.* George Allen & Unwin, London, 1924.

Tyldesley, Joyce. *Ramesses, Egypt's Greatest Pharaoh.* Penguin Books, London, 2001.

--- *Cleopatra, Last Queen of Egypt.* Basic Books, New York, 2008.

Wilkinson, Toby A. H. *Early Dynastic Egypt.* Routledge, London, 1999.

--- *The Rise and Fall of Ancient Egypt: The History of a Civilization from 3000 BC to Cleopatra.* Bloomsbury Publishing, London, 2010.

Image Sources

1. Jeff Dahl, CC BY-SA 4.0 <https://creativecommons.org/licenses/by-sa/4.0>, via Wikimedia Commons: https://commons.wikimedia.org/wiki/File:Eye_of_Ra_bw.svg
2. Dendera_Deckenrelief_02.JPG: Olaf Tauschderivative work: JMCC1 (talk)photographe/égyptologue, CC BY 3.0 <https://creativecommons.org/licenses/by/3.0>, via Wikimedia Commons: https://commons.wikimedia.org/wiki/File:L%27Ogdoade_d%27Hermopolis.jpg
3. Jeff Dahl, CC BY-SA 4.0 <https://creativecommons.org/licenses/by-sa/4.0>, via Wikimedia Commons: https://commons.wikimedia.org/wiki/File:Re-Horakhty.svg
4. Amanda Slater from Coventry, West Midlands, UK, CC BY-SA 2.0 <https://creativecommons.org/licenses/by-sa/2.0>, via Wikimedia Commons: https://commons.wikimedia.org/wiki/File:Tutankhamun_-_Treasures_of_the_Golden_Pharaoh_(49587454536).jpg
5. https://commons.wikimedia.org/wiki/File:Book_of_Gates_Barque_of_Ra_cropped.jpg
6. Eternal Space, CC BY-SA 4.0 <https://creativecommons.org/licenses/by-sa/4.0>, via Wikimedia Commons: https://commons.wikimedia.org/wiki/File:Apep_(Deity).png
7. Eternal Space, CC BY-SA 4.0 <https://creativecommons.org/licenses/by-sa/4.0>, via Wikimedia Commons: https://commons.wikimedia.org/wiki/File:Amun_(God).png
8. https://commons.wikimedia.org/wiki/File:Geb,_Nut,_Shu.jpg
9. Hans Bernhard (Schnobby), CC BY-SA 3.0 <https://creativecommons.org/licenses/by-sa/3.0>, via Wikimedia Commons: https://commons.wikimedia.org/wiki/File:Goddess_Nut_2.JPG
10. Eternal Space, CC BY-SA 4.0 <https://creativecommons.org/licenses/by-sa/4.0>, via Wikimedia Commons: https://commons.wikimedia.org/wiki/File:Set_(God).png

11 P Aculeius, CC BY-SA 3.0 <https://creativecommons.org/licenses/by-sa/3.0>, via Wikimedia Commons: https://commons.wikimedia.org/wiki/File:Sha_(animal).jpg

12 https://commons.wikimedia.org/wiki/File:Set_speared_Apep.jpg

13 derivative work: A. Parrot (talk)La_tombe_de_Horemheb_(KV.57)_(Vallée_des_Rois_Thèbes_ouest)_-4.jpg: Jean-Pierre Dalbéra, CC BY 2.0 <https://creativecommons.org/licenses/by/2.0>, via Wikimedia Commons: https://commons.wikimedia.org/wiki/File:La_Tombe_de_Horemheb_cropped.jpg

14 https://commons.wikimedia.org/wiki/File:The_judgement_of_the_dead_in_the_presence_of_Osiris.jpg

15 Louvre Museum, CC BY-SA 2.0 FR <https://creativecommons.org/licenses/by-sa/2.0/fr/deed.en>, via Wikimedia Commons: https://commons.wikimedia.org/wiki/File:Jewel_Osiris_family-E_6204-IMG_0641-gradient.jpg

16 Jeff Dahl, CC BY-SA 4.0 <https://creativecommons.org/licenses/by-sa/4.0>, via Wikimedia Commons: https://commons.wikimedia.org/wiki/File:Vulture_Crown.png

17 EternalSpace1977, CC BY-SA 4.0 <https://creativecommons.org/licenses/by-sa/4.0>, via Wikimedia Commons: https://commons.wikimedia.org/wiki/File:Isis_(goddess).png

18 Diego Delso, CC BY-SA 4.0 <https://creativecommons.org/licenses/by-sa/4.0>, via Wikimedia Commons: https://commons.wikimedia.org/wiki/File:File,_Asu%C3%A1n,_Egipto,_2022-04-01,_DD_89.jpg

19 Gary Todd from Xinzheng, China, CC0, via Wikimedia Commons: https://commons.wikimedia.org/wiki/File:Ancient_Egypt_Alabaster_Canopic_Jars_(27799088613).jpg

20 Allan Gluck, permissions ticket #2022102610001032, CC BY-SA 4.0 <https://creativecommons.org/licenses/by-sa/4.0>, via Wikimedia Commons: https://commons.wikimedia.org/wiki/File:Mummy_mask_cartonnage_Manchester_Museum_AN_6286_(2).jpg

21 https://commons.wikimedia.org/wiki/File:Anubis_attending_the_mummy_of_Sennedjem.jpg

22 https://commons.wikimedia.org/wiki/File:Egypt_dauingevekten.jpg

23 Eternal Space, CC BY-SA 4.0 <https://creativecommons.org/licenses/by-sa/4.0>, via Wikimedia Commons: https://commons.wikimedia.org/wiki/File:Maat_(Goddess).png

24 https://commons.wikimedia.org/wiki/File:Ammit_BD.jpg

25 https://commons.wikimedia.org/wiki/File:27.1_Iaru.tif

26 https://commons.wikimedia.org/wiki/File:Thoout,_Thoth_Deux_fois_Grand,_le_Second_Herm%C3%A9s,_N372.2A.jpg

27 Jeff Dahl, CC BY-SA 4.0 <https://creativecommons.org/licenses/by-sa/4.0>, via Wikimedia Commons: https://commons.wikimedia.org/wiki/File:Horus_standing.svg

28 https://commons.wikimedia.org/wiki/File:Contendings_of_Horus_and_Seth_(CBL_Pap_1.2).jpg

29 https://commons.wikimedia.org/wiki/File:Statuettes_Senusret_I_Petrie.jpg

30 Jeff Dahl, CC BY-SA 4.0 <https://creativecommons.org/licenses/by-sa/4.0>, via Wikimedia Commons: https://commons.wikimedia.org/wiki/File:Double_crown.svg

31 Bjørn Christian Tørrissen, CC BY-SA 3.0 <https://creativecommons.org/licenses/by-sa/3.0>, via Wikimedia Commons: https://commons.wikimedia.org/wiki/File:Mask_of_Tutankhamun_2003-12-07.jpg

32 RootOfAllLight, CC BY 4.0 <https://creativecommons.org/licenses/by/4.0>, via Wikimedia Commons: https://commons.wikimedia.org/wiki/File:Wadjet_(Deity).svg

33 Onceinawhile, CC BY-SA 4.0 <https://creativecommons.org/licenses/by-sa/4.0>, via Wikimedia Commons: https://commons.wikimedia.org/wiki/File:Tomb_of_Nefertari_2022_57.jpg

34 Nekhbet, CC BY-SA 4.0 <https://creativecommons.org/licenses/by-sa/4.0>, via Wikimedia Commons: https://commons.wikimedia.org/wiki/File:Nekhbet_(Goddess).svg

35 Hedwig Storch, CC BY-SA 3.0 <https://creativecommons.org/licenses/by-sa/3.0>, via Wikimedia Commons: https://commons.wikimedia.org/wiki/File:Kom_Ombo,_Sobek_0319.JPG

36 JMCC1, CC BY-SA 3.0 <https://creativecommons.org/licenses/by-sa/3.0>, via Wikimedia Commons: https://commons.wikimedia.org/wiki/File:The_Crocodile_Museum_0288_b1.jpg

37 https://commons.wikimedia.org/wiki/File:Luxor_temple_16.jpg

38 Jeff Dahl, CC BY-SA 4.0 <https://creativecommons.org/licenses/by-sa/4.0>, via Wikimedia Commons: https://commons.wikimedia.org/wiki/File:Khnum.svg

39 Roland Unger, CC BY-SA 3.0 <https://creativecommons.org/licenses/by-sa/3.0>, via Wikimedia Commons: https://commons.wikimedia.org/wiki/File:DendaraMamisiKhnum-10.jpg

40 The Tomb of Nefetari, CC BY-SA 4.0 <https://creativecommons.org/licenses/by-sa/4.0>, via Wikimedia Commons: https://commons.wikimedia.org/wiki/File:Serket_Tomb_of_Nefetari.png

41 https://commons.wikimedia.org/wiki/File:Egyptian_-_Figure_of_Isis-Serget_as_Scorpion_-_Walters_54546_-_Side_A_(cropped).jpg

42 Heshbi, CC BY-SA 4.0 <https://creativecommons.org/licenses/by-sa/4.0>, via Wikimedia Commons: https://commons.wikimedia.org/wiki/File:Babi_(Egyptian_god).png

43 Senix at English Wikipedia, CC BY 3.0 <https://creativecommons.org/licenses/by/3.0>, via Wikimedia Commons; https://commons.wikimedia.org/wiki/File:Louvre_Serekh.png

44 https://commons.wikimedia.org/wiki/File:Narmer_Palette.jpg

45 Louvre Museum, CC BY 3.0 <https://creativecommons.org/licenses/by/3.0>, via Wikimedia Commons; https://commons.wikimedia.org/w/index.php?curid=17156681

46 Roland Unger, CC BY-SA 3.0 <https://creativecommons.org/licenses/by-sa/3.0>, via Wikimedia Commons; https://commons.wikimedia.org/wiki/File:CairoEgMuseumTaaMaskMostlyPhotographed.jpg

47 https://commons.wikimedia.org/wiki/File:Menkaura.jpg

48 https://commons.wikimedia.org/wiki/File:Sequenre_tao.JPG

49 Ian Lloyd, CC BY-SA 3.0 <https://creativecommons.org/licenses/by-sa/3.0>, via Wikimedia Commons; https://commons.wikimedia.org/wiki/File:Hatshetsup-temple-1by7.jpg

50 https://commons.wikimedia.org/wiki/File:La_salle_dAkhenaton_(1356-1340_av_J.C.)_(Mus%C3%A9e_du_Caire)_(2076972086).jpg

51 William Henry Goodyear, Joseph Hawkes, and John McKecknie, No restrictions, via Wikimedia Commons; https://commons.wikimedia.org/wiki/File:S10.08_Abu_Simbel,_image_9930.jpg

52 https://commons.wikimedia.org/wiki/File:Mummy_Nodjmet_Smith.JPG

53 https://commons.wikimedia.org/wiki/File:Ring_with_engraved_portrait_of_Ptolemy_VI_Philometor_(3rd%E2%80%932nd_century_BCE)_-_2009.jpg

54 Stephen McKay, CC BY-SA 2.0; https://commons.wikimedia.org/wiki/File:Greater_London_House,_Camden_Town_-_geograph.org.uk_-_319426.jpg

www.ingramcontent.com/pod-product-compliance
Lightning Source LLC
Chambersburg PA
CBHW070326010526
44107CB00004B/436